DATE

NOTE

Oxford Historical Monographs will consist of books which would formerly have been published in the Oxford Historical Series. As with the previous series, they will be carefully selected studies which have been submitted, or are based upon theses submitted, for higher degrees in this University. The works listed below are those still in print in the Oxford Historical Series.

THE
General Election
of 1880

BY

TREVOR OWEN LLOYD

OXFORD UNIVERSITY PRESS
1968

Oxford University Press, Ely House, London W. 1

GLASGOW NEW YORK TORONTO MELBOURNE WELLINGTON
CAPE TOWN SALISBURY IBADAN NAIROBI LUSAKA ADDIS ABABA
BOMBAY CALCUTTA MADRAS KARACHI LAHORE DACCA
KUALA LUMPUR HONG KONG TOKYO

PRINTED IN GREAT BRITAIN

ACKNOWLEDGEMENTS

THIS book is an investigation of the General Election of 1880 along the lines of the Nuffield accounts of elections in Britain since 1945. Inevitably past events cannot be studied in the same way as contemporary events, and in any case a nineteenth-century election was not the same thing as a twentieth-century election. But, differences and difficulties apart, the approach is psephological and starts from the premiss that general elections are too important to be left to the politicians.

I originally studied the subject for a doctoral thesis. I was fortunate enough to be a Student at Nuffield College with easy access to the College Library, and also to have two kind and stimulating supervisors, Dr. D. E. Butler and Mr. R. B. McCallum. I used material from the National Liberal Club, from Liberal party headquarters, and from the records at the Conservative Central Office, and found the politicians helpful and co-operative. I also used material from the British Museum, from the Public Record Office, and from Christ Church Library. I am grateful to the present Lord Salisbury, the present Lord Granville, Mr. Charles Gladstone, and the trustees of the Beaconsfield Papers for permission to use material for which they hold the copyright.

In the work of shortening the thesis and rearranging it into a more digestible shape, I benefited from the advice of Professor N. H. Gibbs, and I have been financially assisted by grants from the University of Toronto and the Canada Council.

CONTENTS

I

THE LIBERAL VICTORY

THE election of 1880 is a landmark in nineteenth-century history. It also provides an opportunity for testing a general theory of electoral behaviour. The theory, which has no claim to novelty, runs like this: the electorate at large is not very interested in politics, tends to use its right to vote as a defensive weapon to protect itself against having unpleasant things done to it, and places a loss of economic prosperity high on the list of things it wants to avoid. However, a merely materialist political programme will have relatively little effect: the electorate is not easy to organize without the assistance of enthusiastic political workers, unpaid for the most part, who serve their party out of conviction and make up for the ordinary man's lack of interest. These party workers have to be inspired to spend time on boring and tiresome jobs, and they are very responsive to idealistic sentiments. Ordinary voters are never very interested in foreign or colonial policy, but the party enthusiasts often find that for them the main political issues lie in these fields. Accordingly a political programme should contain material benefits for the ordinary voters, 'each of whom counts for one' at the ballot box, and a more altruistic appeal for the party enthusiasts, each of whom counts for more than one in the eyes of the party managers.

This theory does not explain everything about twentieth-century elections but it clearly could be offered as an account of modern conditions. Equally clearly, it would not be much use as an explanation of an eighteenth-century election. A widely contested late nineteenth-century election provides an opportunity to test or to illustrate the theory; there does seem to be a case for saying that the Liberals owed their great victory in 1880 to a judicious combination of appeals to political enthusiasts over the Eastern crisis of the late seventies and other foreign policy issues with appeals to the electorate to vote against the government because it was responsible for the depression in trade.

Testing the validity of this view is not just a matter of seeing what was said in the election, nor would it be completely settled by investigating the much more difficult question of what the audiences thought when they listened to speeches. Recent books by Professor Gash, Professor Hanham, and others have reminded us how much of the old structure of politics survived the 1832 and even the 1867 Reform Bill.[1] To be able to say very much about the dynamics of an election, it is necessary to look at the social background and see how much of the eighteenth-century framework of dominance by established social groups with no great interest in politics and political principle had survived from the world as it was at the accession of George III.

Some changes had happened. The followers of Lord Grey who passed the 1832 Reform Bill had accepted the principles of Peace, Retrenchment, and Reform—a slogan that fitted the tactical requirements suggested at the end of our first paragraph—and the Liberal party continued to attach some value to these principles in later elections. The differing, though not yet conflicting, interests of the various sections of the Whig-Liberal party found satisfaction in Lord Grey's slogan throughout the period of its dominance from the 1832 to the 1884 Reform Bill, and in 1880 Gladstone based a good deal of the Midlothian campaign on the principles behind the slogan.

Midlothian is a phenomenon to puzzle anyone who argues that social influence, often assisted by corruption and intimidation, remained dominant in nineteenth-century elections. It is also a phenomenon to be considered by contemporary observers who say that very few people are interested in foreign policy and that the way to win an election is to concentrate on domestic affairs and promise material benefits. The success of the Midlothian campaign and its contribution to the general Liberal triumph have been mentioned often enough by historians to make it necessary to try to

[1] N. Gash, *Politics in the Age of Peel* (London, 1953); H. J. Hanham, *Election and Party Management* (London, 1959). W. B. Gwynn, *Democracy and the Cost of Politics* (London, 1962), suggests that this picture of continuity is slightly overdrawn.

explain the cogs and gears and levers by which Gladstone's speeches had an effect over the whole country. We do not at present expect the course of elections to be greatly altered by election speeches, and the effect of Midlothian needs careful assessment.

It seems easiest to study the election by first outlining what happened, and then looking at the factors, some of them familiar to students of twentieth-century politics and some of them more explicable in eighteenth-century terms, that affected the result. This involves a sketch of events a little before the election to show what was at stake, and a reference to the aftermath, in which Gladstone's predominance was recognized by his appointment as Prime Minister although he was not leader of the Liberal party during the election. The events that brought him back to power may be taken to begin with the awakening of public interest in the Eastern question in the summer of 1876, but the story must go back to the general election of 1874.

Gladstone's great ministry of 1868 had begun with a solid and substantial majority united by a desire to disestablish the Church of England in Ireland. Each of the different groups that made up the Liberal party had expected some benefit from Disestablishment, and had taken the inclusion of the measure in the party programme as a sign that their own special interests would receive consideration. But while Disestablishment would appeal to nonconformists, Whig Irish landlords, supporters of efficiency, opponents of vested interests, and prudent members of the Church of England who had no great appetite for defending the indefensible, the later measures of Gladstone's ministry had no such unifying effect. Many abuses were swept away, but those who had suffered from an abuse thought its abolition no more than common justice, and those who had benefited from it were convinced that they had been deprived of their rights.

Two issues caused particular difficulty. The Licensing Act of 1872 convinced brewers, distillers, and pubkeepers that the Liberals were their enemies. People in 'the Trade' had tended to be Liberals, like most of the rest of the manufacturing interest; steadily they became better organized politically and more inclined to be Conservative as the

Liberal party seemed increasingly ready to take up Temperance proposals. Forster's Education Act of 1870 annoyed both the Churchmen and the nonconformists; from the standpoint of a century later, the long-term social importance of the Act was that it laid down that schools should be made available for children throughout the country, but at the time its explosive political implications lay in the fact that it annoyed nonconformists by granting financial assistance to Church of England schools and annoyed the Church of England by establishing a public system of education on a basis of non-denominational Christianity which gave no special recognition to the place of the Established Church.

The Church of England rallied to the Conservative party; the non-conformists set up the National Education League, which ran candidates against the official Liberal candidates at by-elections and at a few places in the general election. There were other 'harassed interests'—trade unionists, Irish landlords and the universities of Oxford and Cambridge all felt ill-treated by the government—but there is a good deal in the view that the Liberals were defeated by Beer and the Bible. Gladstone gave the simpler explanation 'We were swept away in a torrent of gin and beer' (a view he retained in 1880), but this seems to underestimate the importance of education as an issue.[1]

One of Gladstone's remaining political ambitions was to abolish the income-tax; when he proposed this to his Cabinet, the service ministers made it clear that this step would

---

[1] Sir Edward Baines, the most prominent of the Leeds Liberals, wrote down thirteen reasons for defeat. They include the reasons listed above, and a few minor issues. The only issues which were not nation-wide were those that affected the City of London and the dockyards. The list is printed, John Vincent, *The Formation of the Liberal Party* (London, 1966), pp. 124–6. Vincent's own view that, 'It took the Midlothian campaign and a centralised election-fighting machine to impose party discipline on the sophisticated and wilful public opinion of Leeds' (and a number of other large towns) also deserves consideration. The Webbs said, 'It will be a question for the historian of English politics whether the unexpected rout of the Liberal party at the election of 1874 was not due more to the active hostility of the Trade Unionists than to the sullen abstention of the Nonconformists': S. and B. Webb, *The History of Trade Unionism* (London, 1902), p. 270. So far as can be seen from the effect of candidates put forward, the Trade Unionists did little harm to the Liberals. Eleven seats were lost by the Liberals because too many candidates came forward. Only three of these candidates were claimed by the Webbs as supporters of the Trade Unions.

involve such large cuts in the defence estimates that they would prefer a general election beforehand, to cover their position.[1] Gladstone dissolved, and in February 1874 the Liberals were defeated. Disraeli formed the first Conservative ministry with a majority in the Commons since 1846. His personal contribution to the victory had been considerable: with the assistance of Gorst he had modernized the party, found candidates, and made changes in the organization which recognized the impact of the Second Reform Bill; he had picked up some of the Palmerstonian supporters of a strong foreign policy, partly because of his own speeches and partly because the government had leaned too far in a 'Little England' direction; he had committed his party to taking some interest in social reform. The great prosperity of the early seventies might have been expected to help the government, but it seems that public opinion would have preferred to see the government use its surpluses for social improvement rather than removal of the income-tax.

The Conservatives' majority rested on their predominance in England:

	England		Wales		Scotland		Ireland			Total[2]		
	Lib.	Con.	Lib.	Con.	Lib.	Con.	Lib.	HR	Con.	Lib.	HR	Con.
1868	240	223	22	8	52	8	65		40	379		279
1874	171	288	19	11	40	20	13	57	33	243	57	352

In Ireland the Home Rule party, under the gentle ex-Orangeman Butt, gained a great deal of ground, though it was not yet the firmly disciplined party of the eighties.[3] Parnell did not enter Parliament until a by-election in April 1875.

Some of his followers thought the election justified Disraeli's faith in the Conservative working man. Perhaps it

---

[1] It has been suggested (e.g. R. C. K. Ensor, *England 1870–1914* (London, 1946), pp. 25–26) that Gladstone dissolved because he might have had to submit himself for re-election at Greenwich. See *Annual Register for 1874*, p. 2. Like W. H. Maehl, in 'Gladstone, the Liberals and the General Election of 1874', *Bulletin of the Institute of Historical Research*, 1963, p. 53, I have followed Gladstone's own account: Add. MSS. 44790, f. 111.

[2] Four English and two Irish seats had been disfranchised since 1868.

[3] 'Ireland: her Present and her Future', *Edinburgh Review*, Jan. 1880, quotes A. M. Sullivan, the Home Rule M.P., to the effect that the Ballot helped Home Rule even more than the leaders had expected.

also demonstrated the swing of the pendulum. Until 1867 the parties represented two groups in the property-owning classes, landlords and manufacturers. The manufacturers, who were predominantly nonconformist in religion, did not yet aspire to govern the country themselves, and they accepted the leadership of the Whig minority of the land-owning classes. The Whigs were rich, Erastian, and closely connected by intermarriage, and this distinguished them from the bulk of the land-owning class, which was Tory and a little more devoutly Anglican.

The borough householders introduced into the relatively cosy circle of the enfranchised were not natural allies of either group. Lowe asked, during the Reform Bill debates, 'Will they [the political parties] not be totally and entirely altered? They will not be advocates of principle but sup-pliants for popular favour.'[1] He could have reminded him-self by reading his own speeches that the pre-1867 parties had not always adhered to principle, but it was true that after 1867 there was a much less stable political balance than before.

In 1874 there was widespread relief that politics would become less exciting. Gladstone turned his mind to thoughts of retirement and at the beginning of the 1875 session he resigned the leadership of the Liberal party to Lord Gran-ville.[2] Forster and Lord Hartington were regarded as the likeliest candidates for the Liberal leadership in the Com-mons, although neither of them was likely to be very im-pressive. Forster wanted the post, but was disliked by the Radicals because of the Education Act and by the moderates because he was a Radical. Hartington did not want the post, but was pushed into it and did the job much better than had been expected.[3]

Disraeli gave the Conservative leadership in the Commons to Northcote in August 1876, though he later said he would not have gone to the Lords at that time if he had thought Gladstone's retirement would not be permanent.[4] The social

[1] 3 Hansard, clxxxvii. 798. Debate of 20 May 1867.
[2] Gladstone to Granville, 13 Jan. 1875: P.R.O. 30-29-29.
[3] The Gladstone-Granville Correspondence (Camden Society), ii. 464-9.
[4] W. S. Churchill, Lord Randolph Churchill (London, 1951), p. 131.

legislation of the first two years of the new government was not controversial enough to disturb the political scene, and this helps explain why it was not very important as an issue in the election. Acts were passed to tie up loose ends in the Gladstonian legislation. Picketing was legalized and Trade Unions were given a more secure hold on their funds, regimental exchanges were made purchasable, and a few provisions of the Licensing Act were relaxed. One or two attempts were made to change the Education Act in a way that would benefit the Church of England and while very little came of them they did show nonconformists that there were disadvantages about a Conservative government.[1] The issue did not come up in the general election.

Of the larger measures associated with the opening phase of the Conservative ministry, the Public Health Act was concerned with codifying previous legislation and extending the practices of the better municipalities to the whole country, the Artisans' Dwellings Act was legislation giving municipalities powers rather than duties in the field of housing, and the Agricultural Holdings Act, which required a landlord to pay for improvements carried out by a departing tenant allowed him to declare in the contract that he would not pay compensation. This was not very exciting legislation and it is not surprising to find that much more attention was paid to ecclesiastical matters.[2] The Public Worship Regulation Act, passed in 1875 against the opposition of Gladstone and a few other Liberals, was not a very sensible step. The Ritualists, whom it was intended to check, went to prison rather than give up their practices and a number of non-Ritualist clergy felt that this secular intervention was a threat to the whole High Church position. Another question that distracted people from politics was the doctrine of Papal Infallibility; in retirement Gladstone wrote a pamphlet denouncing the decrees of the Vatican Council on the subject, and the public discussion that followed was as fierce as anything prompted by political affairs.

[1] 'Liberal Principles', National Liberal Club pamphlets, vol. 6110.

[2] Cross pointed to what had been done in Birmingham under the Artisans' Dwellings Act: *The Times*, 31 Mar. 1880. For the Treasury point of view, see *Annual Review of 1878*, p. 38. For criticism of the Agricultural Holdings Act, see G. C. Brodrick, *English Land and English Landlords* (London, 1881), pp. 206–10.

Mr. Shannon has recently shown the close connexion between religion and politics in England in the opening stages of the Eastern crisis, and pointed out in particular that nonconformists and High Churchmen came together once the question of atrocities had been raised.[1] It appears that these two groups which could feel themselves persecuted inside England were the section of ecclesiastical society which found it easiest to sympathize with the Balkan Christians and hardest to approve of the traditional pro-Turkish policy followed by the government.

The government had given diplomatic support to Turkey before the agitation began by declining to associate itself with the Berlin Memorandum of May 1876, a programme for Turkish internal reform suggested by the other Powers as a response to revolts in Bosnia and Hercegovina. Disraeli dismissed as 'coffee-house babble' the reports of the *Daily News* that a revolt in Bulgaria had been suppressed with barbarity, and he waved aside suggestions of torture by saying 'oriental people . . . generally terminate their connexion with culprits in a more expeditious way'. This was to seem frivolous and heartless when he had to admit, in his last speech to the Commons, that Baring's Mission of Inquiry had reported that there were 12,000 victims.[2]

Because confirmation of the massacres did not come until the end of the Session of 1876, public anger had to work through pamphlets, the press, and public meetings, and these demonstrations became the characteristic form taken by the Eastern agitation. The tendency to agitation outside Parliament was intensified by the desire of its leaders to exclude politicians, the willingness of almost all the Opposition Front Bench to keep out, and the reluctance of Gladstone to become involved.[3] He was clearly interested;[4] his pamphlet on *Bulgarian Horrors*, published on 6 September, enjoyed an immediate success that placed him at the head

[1] R. T. Shannon, *Gladstone and the Bulgarian Agitation 1876* (London, 1963), pp. 160–90; W. F. Monypenny and G. E. Buckle, *Life of Disraeli* (London, 1920), v. 314–30.

[2] *Daily News*, 23 June 1876; Monypenny and Buckle, op. cit. vi. 42–46.

[3] Shannon, op. cit., pp. 110–12; G. C. Thompson, *Public Opinion and Lord Beaconsfield*, 1875–80 (London, 1886), i. 364.

[4] Gladstone to Granville, 28 Aug. 1876: P.R.O. 30–29–29.

of those who thought the Turkish government should be expelled from Europe 'bag and baggage', but it was never certain that he intended to remain at their head.

For about six weeks the country was as excited as if an election was on. The pressure of opinion, expressed in resolutions passed at meetings to urge the government to help the Balkan Christians, might have affected the Cabinet if it had not been for the Prime Minister's determination. In September he admitted that it would be affectation to pretend that the government's policy was what the people wanted at that moment, but by November he thought his position secure enough to say there was 'no country as well prepared for war as our own'—presumably a war for Turkey and against Russia.[1]

The extra-parliamentary agitation came to a climax on 8 December when thirty-two speakers harangued a large audience in St. James's Hall at a meeting primarily intended to persuade Lord Salisbury, the British delegate to the Constantinople conference, to support the policy of forcing Turkey to reform. The Liberal Front Bench, except Gladstone, did not attend but as eighty-eight of the conveners of the conference were Liberal M.P.s (only one was a Conservative) and fourteen of the speakers were Liberal M.P.s (with no Conservatives), the agitation had clearly lost its non-partisan nature. It had brought Gladstone back to politics as the champion of the Balkan Christians and of the idea of the Concert of Europe—the idea of joint enforcement of reform in Turkey—and it had brought him back as a leader of members of the Liberal party.[2] He could not obtain the support of the whole party for an interventionist policy, and in the resolution on the Eastern Question he moved on 7 May 1877 he did not ask for more than an expression of disapproval of Turkey. Meanwhile the Conservatives, although still divided into pro-Turks under Beaconsfield,

[1] H. Jephson, *The Platform* (London, 1892), ii. 483–95; Thompson, op. cit. i. 382–417.

[2] Shannon, op. cit., p. 260; 'Report of the Conference on the Eastern Question', National Liberal Club pamphlets, vol. 6497. The Duke of Westminster, one of the organizers of the Conference, agreed with Granville that the Liberal Front Bench ought not to appear. Granville to Gladstone, 27 Nov. 1876: Add. MSS. 44171, ff. 21–24.

anti-interventionists under Derby, and pro-Christians under Salisbury, were moving towards Beaconsfield's position, and this tendency was increased when Russia went to war with Turkey and began to advance on Constantinople.

Anti-Turkish feeling was by no means dead, and was taken up by the great Birmingham political organizer Joseph Chamberlain, who used it to launch the National Liberal Federation, a new political body designed to meet the demands of politics after the Second Reform Bill. In December 1877 it was clear that Beaconsfield could not hold his party together in a policy of intervention on the side of Turkey.[1] However, after the Turks had admitted defeat and had accepted the very unfavourable Treaty of San Stefano the Prime Minister was able to gather most of his colleagues behind an anti-Russian policy; when Derby resigned, at the end of March 1878, for fear that this policy would lead to war, Salisbury took his place and immediately put out a statement indicating the points at which the British government found the Treaty unsatisfactory. Diplomatic manœuvring, combined with some quite brisk displays of readiness to use force, pushed the Russian government back to a position where it made a secret agreement with the British to give up some of its gains. Another secret agreement established Turkish acceptance that these revisions were adequate. Once these preparations had been made, the Powers could go to Berlin with some confidence that a satisfactory settlement would be reached.

The official British position had changed during the year or so leading up to Berlin. At first the government tried to maintain the integrity of Turkey and keep her borders unaltered. After San Stefano it was clear that Russia, or her supposed satellite Bulgaria, was bound to make some gains at Turkey's expense, and the issue became one of finding compensation for other Powers which felt they had an interest in the Eastern Question. For this reason Austria was given effective control over Bosnia and Hercegovina and Britain was given effective control over Cyprus. Beaconsfield's great

[1] Carnarvon, Derby, and Salisbury presented their resignations. Beaconsfield felt uncertain about his ability to carry on: Beaconsfield to the Queen, 17 Dec. 1877; Monypenny and Buckle, op. cit. vi. 204-5.

welcome on his return showed that London believed he had
brought back 'peace with honour' and probably the rest of
the country agreed.[1] In the Commons there was a majority
of 143 in favour of the Treaties, which showed that approval
went beyond the Conservative party. Morley wrote, 'it was
the common talk at the moment that if Lord Beaconsfield
had only chosen to dissolve, his majority would have been
safe'.[2] This seems likely, though it would have been unusual
to dissolve in the fourth year of a Parliament in which the
government's majority was unbroken. One Tory journal did
suggest after the election that the Berlin triumph would not
have had time to sink into people's minds in 1878.[3]

The Congress of Berlin brought the middle period of the
Conservative government's term of office to a triumphant
conclusion. There were few successes in the last period of its
term. During the summer of 1878 attention turned to
Afghanistan and to South Africa, and in neither place did
the government emerge well. While the Congress was sitting
at Berlin the Emir of Afghanistan rather unwillingly received
a Russian envoy.[4] To maintain the diplomatic balance Sir
Louis Cavagnari was established as an envoy at Kabul. In
September 1879 the inhabitants rose and massacred him and
his staff. Roberts marched forward to occupy Kabul and
restore British prestige but, as Gladstone pointed out, such
a policy almost inevitably became a matter of burning down
houses and turning families out into the snow. Up till April
1880 Roberts had done the government more harm than
good; it was reported that he had been hanging Afghan
prisoners,[5] and it was only after the election that his march
to Kandahar restored British authority along the frontier.

---

[1] Ibid. vi. 345–9. Salisbury is said to have distrusted the enthusiasm and to have
prophesied trouble at the polls: Lady G. Cecil, *Life of Lord Salisbury* (London,
1921–32), ii. 296.

[2] J. Morley, *Life of Gladstone* (London, 1908), ii. 140.

[3] 'The New Ministry', *Blackwood's Magazine*, June 1880.

[4] For Afghanistan, see speeches of Cranbrook, Childers, and Argyll, in *The
Times*, 21, 28, and 29 Nov., 1878; 'Speech of Cranbrook' printed as *National Union
Pamphlet*, no. 38, and 'Government Policy in Afghanistan', *National Union
Pamphlet*, no. 46; 'The Credentials of the Opposition', *Quarterly Review*, Jan.
1880; and 'Our Afghan Policy', National Liberal Club pamphlets, vol. 6085,
Gladstone's speech of 26 Nov. 1879: *Speeches in Scotland* (London, Edinburgh,
1879–80), i. 47.

[5] *Truth*, 8 and 15 Jan. and 12 Feb. 1880.

Carnarvon's policy of confederation for South Africa attracted little attention in England. In January 1879 the government found itself committed to a native war. The Governor, Sir Bartle Frere, acting on imprecisely expressed instructions, launched a preventive war against the Zulus. The government censured him but did not recall him, a policy which was hard to defend in the Commons.[1] Although the Zulus were eventually crushed at Ulundi in July 1879, the government suffered because one force was annihilated at Isandhlwana and another had to fight a desperate defensive action at Rorke's Drift. Shortly before the election it was reported that British troops had got out of hand in Zululand and in the Transvaal.[2]

Military discipline had been discussed in Parliament in the 1879 session. The Radicals and Home Rulers had strenuously resisted a codifying Bill for military law that retained flogging. On the other side Salisbury noted that any attempt to give up this Bill, or any substantial part of it, would split the Conservative party in two. After a clash in which Chamberlain referred to Hartington as 'lately the leader of the Opposition, but now the leader of a section only', the moderate Liberals fell in behind the more extreme wing. The Conservative attitude was that of people with connexions among army officers, the Radical and Home Rule attitude was that of people who knew that many of their constituents had relations in the ranks who were liable to be flogged.[3]

Economic forces also told against the government. The 1873 boom ended while the Liberals were still in power, and the Conservatives held office against a background of depression. Wages fell fairly steadily, and 1879 saw the highest level of unemployment, among workers eligible to receive benefit from their unions, for the whole period for which this is a useful index—electorally, it was a particularly good index of the position of the enfranchised section of the working class. There were bad harvests in 1873, 1875, 1876,

[1] Gladstone's speech of 25 Nov. 1879: *Speeches in Scotland*, i. 18.
[2] Russell's report in the *Daily Telegraph*, 10 Feb.
[3] Salisbury to Beaconsfield, 5 July 1879: Christ Church papers; J. L. Garvin, *Life of Joseph Chamberlain* (London, 1932) i. 271–2.

and 1877, and in 1879 a very bad summer was followed by low wheat prices, a sign that American grain was beginning to flow along the railway lines built in the early seventies. Protectionists began to argue that Britain might force other countries to grant tariff concessions by putting up a tariff wall of her own, and in 1879 Salisbury came close to expressing approval of this policy. Northcote claimed he was imposing as little new taxation as possible, but the level of income-tax rose from twopence in 1874 to threepence in 1876 and fivepence in 1878.[1]

Once the Eastern crisis was over, Gladstone slipped back a little from the centre of the stage. However, at the beginning of 1879 he accepted an invitation to stand for the Scottish county of Midlothian or Edinburghshire which was regarded as controlled by the Tory Duke of Buccleugh, although it had been won by the Liberals in 1868. Gladstone arranged to make a preliminary series of speeches in his new constituency in November and December of 1879. This first Midlothian campaign had a considerable effect on the relative standing of politicians and, so far as can be seen, made a great impression on the electorate.[2]

At the beginning of November *Punch* published a cartoon, in which Gladstone was not included, of leading politicians drawn as cocks crowing or about to crow. Two mass meetings had been held in Manchester: on Friday, 17 October Salisbury met the Chamber of Commerce and then spoke to 700 Lancashire Conservatives at a banquet, and the next day he addressed 12,000 people at the Pomona Gardens and said a few words afterwards to 20,000 people outside the Gardens. On 24 October Hartington dissected Salisbury's speech at a banquet and the next day he made a short speech and Bright made a full-scale speech to 20,000 people in the Pomona Gardens. After this both Bright and Hartington made short speeches to 50,000 people outside the Gardens. Many other speeches were made during the recess—more speeches by Cabinet ministers and ex-Cabinet ministers, it

---

[1] J. Clapham, *Economic History of Modern Britain* (Cambridge, 1950–2), ii. 379–82 and 452–60. Salisbury's speech, *The Times*, 18 Oct. 1879; Northcote's speech, in 'Conservative Finance and Liberal Fallacies', *National Union Pamphlet*, no. 39.

[2] Adam to Gladstone, 3, 10, 15, 17, and 28, Jan. 1879: Add. MSS. 44095, ff. 70–78. Adam assured Gladstone that the Liberals would win Midlothian.

was estimated, than in all the recesses of other Parliaments put together. One speech by a backbencher gained the attention always attracted by a politician who attacks his own party: Cowen the Radical Member for Newcastle declared his belief that intervention in the East had been justified, and his speech was reprinted for circulation by the National Union of Conservative Associations.[1]

Gladstone's first visit to Midlothian, between 24 November and 8 December, dwarfed all this. He reckoned he had addressed 86,930 people, giving nine speeches in his constituency between 24 and 29 November and a further eighteen speeches while touring the Lowlands and returning to Hawarden. The campaign was the great event of the recess. The claim that it swayed the result of the election may be too bold, but it is worth asking if there has been any other set of speeches about which such a claim could even be contemplated.[2] *Punch* devoted its full-page cartoon to Gladstone for three successive weeks and at Christmas, when it showed the leading politicians stirring a plum-pudding, Gladstone and Beaconsfield were the most prominent.[3] When Granville, Hartington, Harcourt, Adam (the Liberal Chief Whip), and Cardwell met to hear Lord Wolverton's report on the Midlothian tour they learnt that Gladstone had not expected it to be so successful and that he saw he might have to reconsider his position. Granville put to Wolverton the point that Gladstone's emergence as leader might frighten away moderate voters, but that if his position remained indefinite the enthusiasts would not feel there was no hope of his return.[4] Even before the Midlothian campaign the Chief Whip had expected a majority of fifty, and after the visit

[1] *Punch*, 1 Nov. 1879; *The Times*, 18, 20, 25, and 27, Oct. 1879. *Annual Register for 1880*, p. 5; *Minutes of 1880 Conference of the National Union.*

[2] Gladstone's memorandum on his audiences: Add. MSS. 44763, ff. 164–5. The Edinburgh Telegraph Department wrote to Gladstone and told him that 800,330 words had been cabled during his campaign, some messages going to as many as sixty-eight addresses (i.e. a news agency service): Add. MSS. 44461, f. 227. Lord George Hamilton reckoned *The Times* printed 85,000 words of Gladstone in the first campaign and a total of a quarter of a million words from Nov. 1879 to Apr. 1880. Speech of 14 Jan., and *Parliamentary Reminiscences and Reflections 1868–1885* (London, 1917), p. 172.

[3] *Punch*, 6, 13, 20, and 27 Dec. 1879.

[4] Wolverton to Gladstone, 17 and 20 Dec. 1879: Add. MSS. 44349, ff. 113–18 and 121–2.

Adam's figures became so optimistic that Granville declined
to believe them. The Liberals' confidence was also raised by
the results of the 1879 municipal elections; these results and
Adam's initial predictions no doubt encouraged Gladstone
to declare that Parliament should be dissolved rather than
be allowed to go into a seventh session in which the election hanging over it might tempt the government to produce
vote-catching legislation.[1]

Beaconsfield, who found it a 'relief that this drenching
rhetoric' had ceased, took no notice of the call to dissolve.
Hicks Beach said he looked forward to a working session,
which presumably meant placing Lord Cairns's codification
of the patent, bankruptcy, and criminal law on the Statute
Book. A Seats Bill was almost introduced on 4 March, and
the form it was rumoured to have taken was advantageous
enough to the government to make it slightly surprising
that Beaconsfield dissolved instead of persevering with the
Bill. Seats were to be created to replace the two English
double-member constituencies of Bewdley and Beverley disenfranchised in 1869 for corruption, and to replace the
disenfranchised Irish single-member constituencies of Cashel
and Sligo. Constituencies said to be likely to get a third seat
included Bradford, Bristol, Newcastle-on-Tyne, and Sheffield
—under the clause of the 1867 Act providing for minority
representation in a three-member constituency, the Conservatives would gain—and it was suggested that Accrington
might get a seat, which would remove from the county
register a strongly Liberal area on which Hartington relied in
his efforts to regain North-East Lancashire. Irish third-member
seats for Dublin, County Cork, and Kingstown were also
mentioned, and might be expected to return Conservatives.[2]

The Bill as described would not be willingly laid aside.
The only new factor which appeared between 4 March and
8 March, when Beaconsfield announced his intention to

[1] See Wolverton to Granville, 3 Nov. 1879: P.R.O. 30–29–27; Gladstone to
Granville, 4 Nov. 1879: P.R.O. 30–29–29; Gladstone's speech of 25 Nov. 1879:
Speeches in Scotland, i. 16.

[2] Monypenny and Buckle, op. cit. vi. 501; *The Times*, 22 Jan.; on the Seats Bill,
The Times, 5 Mar.; *East Suffolk Gazette*, 3 Feb.; *Northampton Mercury*, 14 Feb.;
Manchester Guardian, 25 Feb.; *Exeter and Plymouth Gazette*, 15 Mar.; speech of
Hartington, *The Times*, 15 Mar.

dissolve Parliament, was the gathering of a storm over the Water Bill that had been introduced on 2 March. The Bill was intended to unify the private water companies of London into a single municipal monopoly which could provide a purer and cheaper supply. The rate of compensation was designed to give the shareholders the same income from government bonds at $3\frac{1}{2}$ per cent. as they had previously enjoyed from Water shares yielding 7 per cent.: this meant a capital gain of 100 per cent. The price of Water shares shot up and opinion, even in the Conservative press, hardened against the Bill so much that it was not at all certain to pass. In his election address Hartington mentioned the Water Bill as the latest example of ministerial incompetence, and other people also condemned it on these grounds. The *Daily News*, which had been non-committal when the details of the Water Bill first appeared, became convinced that it was a piece of bungling, and later went further and denounced it as a 'detected job'.[1]

Hartington said that the short session had been held in order to manœuvre the Liberals into appearing to favour Home Rule: the government had introduced changes in parliamentary procedure to check obstruction, and if the Liberals had done anything more than suggest a few improvements, the election would have been fought on the maintenance of the Union. The Liverpool by-election added to the impression that the Liberals could be seen as the party of Home Rule, and the emphasis of Beaconsfield's address also gives some support to this theory about the dissolution.[2]

It has been suggested that the by-election results encouraged Beaconsfield to dissolve, though his letters to the Queen do not support this view.[3] Three by-elections are usually mentioned: Sheffield, Liverpool, and Southwark. At Sheffield in December 1879 the Conservatives had put up a very strong fight for the seat previously held by Roebuck in a constituency they had not even contested in 1874.

[1] See W. M. Torrens, 'The Water Supply of London', *Macmillan's Magazine*, Dec. 1879 (this is not an article for the squeamish); *The Economist*, 24 Jan., and 6 and 13 Mar.; *Standard*, leader of 5 Mar., and letters of 9 Mar. Hartington's address, *The Times*, 11 Mar.; *Daily News*, 12 Mar.

[2] *The Times*, 10 Feb. and (Hartington's speech), 15 Mar.

[3] Beaconsfield to the Queen, 14 Feb.: Monypenny and Buckle, op. cit. vi. 511–12.

However, Roebuck had become a rather Tory sort of Radical by 1874, had received Church and brewing support in the election and had subsequently voted with the government on foreign policy. The seat was in fact narrowly balanced, and after going Liberal at the by-election it went Conservative at the general election.

At Liverpool the Conservatives held the seat, which was the normal result there, and the Liberals made a slight gain in their percentage of the votes cast. While the by-election was on, the Irish supporters of Home Rule asked the Liberal candidate, Lord Ramsay, to pledge himself to vote for an inquiry into the desirability of a Parliament for Ireland. At first he declined but, faced with the loss of the Irish vote, he accepted another pledge that was almost exactly the same. Hartington made it clear that he preferred Liberals not to support an inquiry and that the Liberal party certainly could not support Home Rule.[1] The Conservatives said the election had gone against Ramsay because of his Home Rule views, and of course Home Rule views did awaken strong Orange reaction in Liverpool.

The Southwark by-election had a more clear-cut result. The Liberal organization had been divided for some time. In the past they could select a candidate by arranging that the Liberal who was doing less well at the end of the first hour of voting should stand down, but this arrangement had not been honoured in the 1870 by-election and since then the Conservatives had held one of the seats, though always with a minority of the votes cast. In the 1880 by-election for the Liberal Member's seat, the Conservative candidate, Sir Edward Clarke, polled more votes than the Liberal and the Radical put together.

The Cabinet appears to have considered dissolution immediately after this, but it decided to wait until the Budget had been presented. The change of approach, three weeks later, before the Budget appeared, suggests that the Water Bill rather than the by-elections was decisive, though no doubt the latter encouraged Beaconsfield to think that dissolution was a practicable policy. About the time of the dissolution it seems to have been expected on the Conservative

[1] *The Times*, 26 and 29 Jan., and 10 Feb.

side that the Liberals would gain fairly heavily in Scotland and Ireland, but that only a small number of English seats would change hands.[1] Newspaper opinion coincided with this assessment; it is not clear how far the Liberals also accepted it and how far they had been convinced by Adam's optimism.

A dissolution must have been considered a possibility, but there is every sign that it came as a distinct surprise—and a surprise that did nothing for Beaconsfield's reputation as a serious statesman—when it was announced on 8 March that the Parliament of 1874 had about a fortnight to live.[2] There was still some parliamentary business to complete. A Budget was submitted which, by increasing and reorganizing the Probate Duties to bring in another £700,000, reached a state of approximate balance. Gladstone said the increases hit the moderately well-off and benefited the rich; the Conservatives replied that the Budget was only bringing to an end anomalies for which Gladstone was himself partly responsible. The Liberals left themselves the option, which they later exercised, of replacing the Budget with one of their own but did not interfere with its passage. The government also introduced an Electoral Practices Bill which, in addition to renewing the Ballot Act which was about to expire, allowed candidates to provide free transport to the polling stations in boroughs, thus putting them on the same basis as county constituencies. This was justified on the grounds that nobody took any notice of the prohibition in any case, and it passed into law so far as England was concerned with very little trouble. Scottish and Irish Members successfully insisted that it should not be extended to their countries. By the time the Bill passed into law it was very hard to find a quorum, and the comment of a Liberal Member that the previous election had been fought on beer and the Bible and this one would be fought on cabs and corruption was almost the last thing said in the old House.[3]

Parliament ceased to be the centre of attention when the

[1] Monypenny and Buckle, op. cit. vi. 520; *Daily News*, 19 Mar.; *The Times*, 25 Mar.; 'Public Opinion and its Leaders', *Fortnightly Review*, Aug. 1880.

[2] The decision was taken by the Cabinet on 6 Mar.: Monypenny and Buckle, op. cit. vi. 514. The Conservative *Morning Post*, 9 Mar., seemed to feel that the dissolution needed to be justified. See Gladstone's address, *The Times*, 12 Mar.

[3] 3 *Hansard*, ccli. 1119 and 1134; Anderson's comment, 1212.

election addresses came out. Beaconsfield's, which was published the day after the announcement of the dissolution, was the most graphically written. The *Spectator's* comments, while hostile, contain some valid points: it was probably true that neat alliteration, and ornate phrases about 'peace rests on the presence, not to say the ascendancy of England in the Councils of Europe', made the address attractive to people who would take little interest in anything more conventional. On the other hand the *Standard* thought its language a little too sonorous for a refined taste, the grammarians thought 'men of light and leading' incorrect and Hartington said that the phrase about consolidating co-operation was acceptable to both sides, if not comprehensible to either.[1]

Nobody was sure that a peer should issue a party manifesto. In 1865 Lord Derby, the leader of the Conservatives, had left Disraeli to state the party's case in his address to the electors of Buckinghamshire. In 1880 Beaconsfield launched his manifesto as an Open Letter to the Duke of Marlborough, Lord Lieutenant of Ireland at the time. The choice of recipient was presumably intended to give added force to his attempts to make Irish affairs the important issue in the election. For the long run this was prescient, and the manifesto touched on the issues—Ireland, colonial affairs, and foreign policy—that were to dominate much of British politics for the rest of the century. So far as the election was concerned, his harsh references to Ireland and to Home Rule did his cause no good. He was quite right to calculate that the great Irish landlords among the Whigs such as Hartington and Lansdowne would do their best to check any Liberal moves in the direction of Home Rule. On the other hand, if the Liberals remained uncommitted the Irish might stand neutral or even support the Conservatives because their educational policy was preferable. Beaconsfield's manifesto resolved any doubts the Irish may have had: it insulted Home Rule so violently by calling it 'worse than pestilence and famine' (a form of words that showed little sympathy for the current food shortage in Ireland) that the Irish in England were bound to vote against the Conservatives. The

---

[1] Text of letter to the Duke of Marlborough, *The Times*, 9 Mar.; *Spectator*, 20 Mar.; *Standard*, 10 Mar.; Hartington's comments, *The Times*, 15 Mar.

Irish Home Rule Confederation left them in no doubt about their duty, telling them to 'vote against Benjamin Disraeli as you should vote against the mortal enemy of your country and your race'. The Confederation tried in this way to avoid compromising the Liberals by too open an endorsement but at the same time guided the Irish on to their side. Many Irishmen in England would no doubt have voted against the government in any case, because of depression and because the Liberals were the party of the urban working man, but Beaconsfield might have given his party a better chance of retaining some of the Irish vote if he had expressed himself more temperately.[1]

In general the manifesto attracted attention but did not carry conviction, and it was attacked for omitting some important issues. After dealing with Ireland it went on to say that the current European situation was very dangerous. This was not an issue in which the electorate was very interested. On the Eastern Question there was very little, on trade and finance nothing at all. It was true that foreign policy was one of the main issues, but Beaconsfield was wrong in thinking that people were worried about future foreign policy; it was the past policy of the government that they wanted to discuss. Possibly because he realized this, there were rumours during the campaign that Beaconsfield was planning a second intervention.[2]

Northcote's address came closer to the issues that attracted attention during the campaign. Ignoring Beaconsfield's suggestion that Europe was so unsettled that only a Conservative government could avert war, he told his constituents and the country at large that the government had averted war and that the period of anxiety was consequently coming to an end. The address was unlikely to attract as much attention as Beaconsfield's, if only because the style was pedestrian, but in its explanation of financial questions and its pride that

[1] Address by the Irish Home Rule Confederation, *The Times*, 13 Mar.; further statement by the Home Rule Confederation, *Daily News*, 29 Apr.; speeches by Sullivan, *The Times*, 19 and 26 Mar.; W. Saunders, *The New Parliament of 1880* (London, 1880), p. 159, which includes the statement that the Irish supported the Liberals in 39 out of the 43 English constituencies in which their votes were important.

[2] *Northampton Mercury*, 27 Mar.; *East Suffolk Gazette*, 30 Mar.

England had kept the peace it did face the questions that interested the electorate.[1]

Granville, as a peer, issued no address and left it to Hartington to make the official statement. This might have handicapped the Liberals; in the absence of party platforms the addresses of the leaders had to serve as the best expression of party policy, though they could not be regarded as requests for a mandate. Beaconsfield's faintly unconventional action had provided the Conservatives with a rallying-point; there was a possibility that on the Liberal side Hartington's address would seem to come from a man without full authority or even that it might be overshadowed by Gladstone's. Nothing like this happened. Hartington's address was sound and serious, and helped the increase in his public reputation that was one of the features of the campaign. In criticizing the government he dealt with its incompetence rather than its political immorality but readers were left in no doubt about the warmth of his feelings. Gladstone's address, which appeared the day after Hartington's, was praised for its economical phrasing and for its gravity, and its forceful earnestness threw into relief the effervescence of Beaconsfield's production.[2]

The *Spectator*, which said that the enlarged franchise included many people who liked a striking phrase delivered with authority, seems to have thought the Liberals would suffer from the contrast between the addresses of the leaders of the two parties.[3] But the comparison was not entirely in the government's favour. There was a contrast between the vagueness of Northcote's statement that after the international situation had cleared up it would be 'in the power of the next Parliament to carry on the work of social and domestic improvement with undivided energy' and the statements of Gladstone and Hartington that they would extend the county franchise. The Liberal leaders were also relatively precise in their statements that the country's financial position could be improved; neither Beaconsfield nor Northcote committed themselves on these questions of policy for the future.

[1] Text of Northcote's address, *The Times*, 11 Mar.
[2] Hartington and Gladstone's addresses, *The Times*, 11 and 12 Mar.
[3] *Spectator*, 13 and 20 Mar.

This particular omission was not out of keeping with the course of the election. The electorate seems to have accepted Gladstone's argument that the election should be treated as a great state trial in which the government was prosecuted for its past actions, particularly for its foreign and colonial policy from 1876 onwards. This conception of the struggle lent dignity to the Liberal arguments; an air of small-minded eccentricity had been settling on the Liberal party as it became involved in issues like Temperance, and in addition it had been accused of being unpatriotic. The issue of patriotism was no doubt taken much less seriously by the electorate than the Conservatives imagined, but it could do the Liberals no harm if people were reminded that the Liberal leaders were, and always had been, serious statesmen.

Gladstone and the rest of the more radical wing of the Liberals did moderate their criticisms on foreign policy as the election came nearer.[1] The party continued to put forward the characteristic arguments of a left-wing party: it said that certain legislative changes were necessary, that policy had been dictated too much by expediency and too little by morality, and that the government had shown itself inhumane in its actions. This was in a tradition that runs from Fox to the present day, and Gladstone was an almost ideal representative of this tradition. Hartington was not the best of men for such questions of principle; his particular value to the Liberal party was his ability to put forward moderate arguments for change in a way that made them appear truly conservative.

The newspaper reports speak of Members drafting addresses and sending instructions to agents and committees from the Commons telegraph offices; 400 telegrams were sent in the first hour after the announcement of the dissolution.[2] Relatively little happened in the open in the next few days, though presumably candidates went on polishing their addresses and constituency organizations booked halls for meetings and drew up lists of supporters. Attendance in the Commons did not fall off until the Budget had been presented, and there was no sudden outbreak of speech-making

---

[1] For jeers at this move, *Globe*, 30 Mar.
[2] *The Times*, 9 Mar.

in the constituencies.[1] There were limits on such activities: convention discouraged Members from invading other constituencies while an election was on. This applied in by-elections as well: in 1876 Gladstone declined an invitation to speak in the Buckinghamshire by-election on the grounds that his visit could become an election issue that would benefit the Conservatives, and in 1879 he was accused of undue interference when he spoke in the Chester by-election. After the dissolution he spoke in Marylebone, the constituency of his Harley Street house, and asserted his right to speak by saying, 'You need not be surprised when I tell you that I have come here as an elector and not as a candidate'. He made speeches during his train journey to Midlothian, and also made a speech when his itinerary in his constituency took him to Peebles, though he apologized for speaking outside Midlothian on that occasion. Rosebery wanted to persuade him to go to Wigtownshire, saying the visit might help win Wigtown Burghs, Wigtownshire, South Ayrshire, and Kirkcudbright. Adam doubted the propriety of bringing a stranger to speak in a county, and Gladstone wrote to Granville that he did not think it would do any good, and that in any case he had never been as a stranger into a county and did not like the precedent. Northcote made a speech in Shoreditch Town Hall while his duties as Leader of the House kept him in London. He made a few speeches in his own constituency of North Devon, where he was not opposed, and after his son Henry had been elected in Exeter both of them went to Torquay to help the Conservatives in East Devon. Hartington went to East Derbyshire, where the family influence was strong, and made a speech although the purpose of his visit was to get a day or two of rest.[2]

While Members of the Commons might feel uneasy about speaking outside their own constituencies, peers were much more completely silenced. It was taken to be a principle of Common Law, reinforced by a sessional order of the House of Commons, that they should not interfere in elections.

---

[1] Attendance declined within a week: *Globe*, 16 Mar.

[2] Gladstone to Granville, 27 Aug. 1876: P.R.O. 30-29-29; *Annual Register for 1879*, p. 101; *The Times*, 13, 17, and 31 Mar.; Rosebery to Granville, 25 Mar.: P.R.O. 30-29-27, and Gladstone to Granville, 26 Mar.: P.R.O. 30-29-29. For Northcote and Hartington, see *The Times*, 24 Mar. and 6 Apr.

There were no precedents for speeches being condemned as interference, but it was taken for granted that they did not speak. Granville made use of an engagement to open a Working Men's Club in Hanley to defend the policy of the previous Liberal government and to point out the divergent views on the political situation to be found in the addresses of Beaconsfield and Northcote. The newspapers noted the skill of his remarks and in some cases they also suggested that it was a little like sharp practice for a peer to intervene in such a way.[1] No Conservative peer spoke, which must have been a handicap for the party: Salisbury was ill and out of the country, but Cairns and Cranbrook were very useful platform speakers, and Beaconsfield himself might have achieved a good deal, despite his failing health, if he had been able to take part freely.

The most powerful intervention by a peer was made by their former colleague Lord Derby. He had none of his father's dash and his political stability was not as great as it might have been. Family custom and his father's career had led him into the Conservative party, but his pacific principles had led him to resign the Foreign Secretaryship at a tense moment in the Eastern crisis. He became committed to the Liberal party some time before the election, but made this public only after the dissolution had been announced. His declaration of his position encouraged the Liberals, and the Conservatives were perhaps a little too elaborately unconcerned about it.[2]

Gladstone's journey to his constituency on 16 March was the most spectacular event of the campaign. His Midlothian supporters suggested that a few speeches might be useful, though they spoke of a two-day visit rather than another series of speeches like that of the previous November. Gladstone decided that he would make an effort on the same scale as before and as the first step his train journey was planned carefully, if without too much concern for the convenience of passengers who merely wanted to go to Scotland.

[1] *The Times*, 22 Mar.

[2] The letter appeared in the papers on 15 Mar. Derby to Granville, 28 Oct. 1879, shows that he was already committed to the Liberals: P.R.O. 30–29–27. See the comments of the *Globe* and the *Standard*, 15 Mar.

Handbills were passed round in London telling people to come to King's Cross Station, where he gave the first of the five speeches he made during the day. The train stopped at Grantham, where he spoke fairly informally; at York, where the Mayor and three thousand people had come to hear him speak; at Newcastle, where he tried to smooth down the differences between Joseph Cowen and the Liberal party; and at Berwick. Finally, forty minutes late, the train reached Edinburgh and Gladstone drove off to Rosebery's mansion at Dalmeny.

It was noticed afterwards that the Liberals had gained a seat at every stop where he had spoken, and no doubt even a brief visit would inspire the Liberal party workers. Crowds gathered at other places simply to see the train go past; Gladstone's magnetic power was clearly as great as it had been at any time since his return to politics in 1876. In his speeches on the journey he did not say much about the issues of foreign policy that had inspired him for so long. In these short speeches the Probate Duties in the recent Budget were the most prominent topic. He opened up one wider issue when he said at King's Cross that he was going north to sweep the Conservatives out of Midlothian and, he hoped, out of a great number of other seats as well. There was always something a little unreal about the pretence that he was just a private individual playing his part in the great Liberal army, but at no other time did he come so close to admitting that he was the leader of the army in its onslaught.[1]

The campaign cannot be divided easily into different phases. Once the dissolution had been announced there was no particular day on which activity began or moved into a new level of intensity. Because there were no reliable guides to the way opinion was moving it is impossible to say that it flowed one way in a particular week or that it changed course around a particular day. Nomination day was not the signal for a change of tempo, because candidates were usually nominated the day before polling took place in their constituency. This meant that the only landmark between the

---

[1] All newspapers on 17 Mar. reported the journey in great detail. Herbert Gladstone, *After Thirty Years* (London, 1928), p. 130, gives extracts from his father's diary.

announcement of the forthcoming dissolution and the first results was the formal act of dissolution; there were a few hypersensitive complaints that the Conservatives had timed their dissolution so that they should have a favourable speech from the Throne at the end of the Session as part of their propaganda, but so little notice was taken of the official end of the old Parliament that the speech could hardly have had any effect. The announcement of the first results came closer to marking a phase in the election because, although there was still much to be done, the early results were generally believed to affect the later ones.

It is not easy to demonstrate the existence of this bandwagon effect and the course of developments in the 1885 election, in which the Liberals rallied in the county seats after doing badly in the boroughs, suggests that it may have been exaggerated.[1] Certainly the fact that the election was fought to a considerable extent as 416 separate constituency battles made it hard to find any close unity of action at the national level; this of course was merely the normal pattern of nineteenth-century elections, and this normal pattern makes the nation-wide impact of Gladstone in Midlothian all the more unusual. But neither Gladstone nor any other national leader went on tour during the election and the national press did not provide so firm a background of information that the whole struggle could be followed from *The Times* or the *Daily Telegraph* point of view.

The central party organizations were still closely linked to the Whips' offices and were mainly devoted to securing a good division. At a dissolution the Whips tried to turn themselves into an electoral organization, and during the seventies they had become increasingly concerned with electoral affairs, but neither this nor the growth of national political organizations made the campaigns nation-wide in the modern sense. The difficulty of finding any national unifying forces was increased by the attitude of certain candidates. For instance, the candidates in the City of London might have been expected to set an example of ranging widely over the issues, but instead they devoted a good deal of time to defending the privileges of city corporations.

[1] Redistribution had made it easier for Liberals to win county seats in 1885.

Relatively few candidates spoke so directly on local issues, but then relatively few constituencies had problems that were so likely to be the subject of legislation. Of course candidates benefited from their local popularity, and this might be connected with their attitude to a political issue— the Game Laws were an obvious example—but when J. O. Lever asked the electors of Galway to vote for him because it would help Galway's prosperity to elect a man of his business enterprise, this was considered rather amusing and distinctly unusual.[1]

The absence of a well-disciplined party organization, and the obvious limitations of the other means of publicity available, made it hard to introduce new topics at short notice. This helps explain why Beaconsfield's sudden raising of the Irish issue had so little effect on the course of discussion during the election and it also helps explain why the Eastern Question continued to be so important; the work of driving it into people's minds had been carried out very thoroughly since 1876. The newspapers said that people's minds would not be changed by anything said in election speeches or addresses, and Gladstone seems to have agreed that it took at least a few weeks for speeches to make an impression. He did not decline invitations to other constituencies purely out of respect for the conventions. When he declined the invitation to the Buckinghamshire by-election he advised the Liberals to work along the lines of votes already promised, and get as many as they could by private channels and not rely too much on meetings. When he declined the invitation to Wigtownshire during the election he said, 'I do not believe that any of these speeches act materially at the moment in the place—though I do believe they have a good deal of silent and slower effect on the tone of the public mind generally'.[2]

The Times had put forward, the previous October, a slightly different but not irreconcilable theory of public opinion. Commenting on the Liberals' mass meeting in Manchester, it said that there was a great mass of uncommitted opinion in the centre and that Bright's speech was

---

[1] Saunders, op. cit., pp. 249–50.
[2] See above, Gladstone to Granville, 27 Aug. 1876 and 26 Mar. 1880: P.R.O. 30–29–29.

very good at rousing the meeting but would do nothing to win over the uncommitted voters. While the election was on, *The Times* continued to argue that politicians should woo the centre. However, at other moments in the election it put forward the rather different view that nobody's mind was going to be changed by what was said in election speeches and addresses. Presumably this was closer to what Gladstone meant when he spoke of speeches having no immediate effect, and if the mind of the electorate worked in this way, then it made very good sense for Bright to go out and stir up the enthusiasm of the party workers so that they should in turn bring the less interested voters to the polling-booths.[1]

Enthusiasm was aroused very effectively, and the public interest in the campaign was high: more candidates and more voters appeared than ever before, the party organizations ran as efficiently as before, and there were at least as many speeches and meetings and demonstration of public support as in any previous election. The uproarious performances of open voting and the hustings were not repeated, and the election was conducted in a more serious atmosphere, but this was in no sense a case of organization triumphing over apathy. Such a triumph would have been hard to achieve, because the party organizations had no bureaucracies to enable them to carry on when enthusiasm was declining.

Gladstone in Scotland continued to dominate the election. Before the dissolution the Liberal leaders had been afraid that he might be speaking too frequently and running the risk of wearying his audiences.[2] The events of the election showed that this fear was groundless, both so far as Midlothian audiences were concerned and for the larger audience in the background that followed his speeches in the newspapers. Gladstone's effect must be studied in more detail when considering the issues in dispute at the election and the

---

[1] *The Times*, 27 Oct. 1879 and 27 Mar. 1880, on wooing the centre, can be contrasted with its view of 18 Mar. The *Morning Post*, 12 Mar., also suggested that people would not be affected by the campaigning.

[2] Forster to Granville, 17 Dec. 1879: P.R.O. 30-29-27; Granville to Gladstone, 30 Jan. 1880: Add. MSS. 44172, ff. 11–13.

reasons for its outcome; at this point it is enough to say that the election fitted the pattern he wanted. It was fought as an inquest on the past policy of the government rather than a comparison of policies for the future. He thought an election should be a contest between parties putting forward opposing arguments with all the eloquence at their command; the ways in which the contest fell short of this ideal will be studied in a later chapter, but the ideal was brought some way closer to realization.[1]

The silence of his great rival meant that during the campaign Gladstone did not seem to be taking part in a continuous debate as he had done during the previous four years. The argument between Cross, who was defending South-West Lancashire against an attack reinforced by Lord Derby, and Hartington, who was contesting the Conservative county of North-East Lancashire, had something of the elements of a debate; they made a point of replying to arguments in one another's speeches, though the clash was not as fierce as it might have been if they had visited one another's constituencies. Hartington spoke more often than Gladstone, and Cross only a little less often, but they were not determined enough as debaters to have the same effect as he did. One of the difficulties confronting moderate men struggling for the centre was brought out by the *Spectator*, commenting on the weakness of Cross's attempt to debate: on 20 March he firmly declared, 'I attack you' and then failed to make any forceful attack worth the introduction.[2]

Hartington, like Gladstone, had a seat in reserve while he tried to win a Conservative county. In Gladstone's case the Leeds Liberals had nominated him and gone about the work of getting him elected while he carefully stood aloof; Hartington had retained his Radnor seat to which he had retired when defeated in 1874 (Parnell, it may be noted, was elected for three seats: Cork, co. Mayo, and co. Meath). Hartington's handling of the Irish Question and of the

---

[1] Robert Kelley, 'Midlothian: a Study in Politics and Ideas', *Victorian Studies*, Dec. 1960, pp. 119–40, gives a good concise account of Gladstone's approach.

[2] The contest can be followed in the *Manchester Guardian*: for Cross, 19, 22–26, and 29–31 Mar., 1–3, 5, 8, and 9 Apr.; for Hartington, 15, 23–26, 29, and 30 Mar., 1–3 and 5–8 Apr. *Spectator*, 27 Mar.

Conservative claim that many loyal Liberals supported the government's foreign policy was skilful, but it tended to concentrate on showing that his party was respectable. He was much less convinced than Gladstone that the Liberals ought to produce an alternative foreign policy and Cross was not an intransigent supporter of Beaconsfield's policy, so on this issue both of them were well placed to appeal to the moderates.[1]

Northcote's position made him the Conservative leader who should reply to Gladstone, if anyone was to undertake the task. Perhaps wisely he made no attempt to repeat, before a wider audience, the debate that Cross and Hartington were conducting in Lancashire. Unsuccessful efforts seem to have been made to launch him in a large urban seat as well as his safe county seat; in any case he was busy taking the Budget and the Electoral Practices Act through the Commons and his speech at Shoreditch was unsuccessful. After the dissolution he went to his seat in North Devon; Beaconsfield thought this was useful, because the small towns of the West of England seemed to him to be the area of real danger for the Conservatives, though the results show that this was a misreading of the situation.[2]

Apart from Gladstone and Hartington, the Liberals had Goschen and Lowe to represent the Right, Harcourt and Forster for the moderate Left, and Bright to serve as a link between the Gladstonian Left and the Chamberlainite Left. All of them were distinguished men who broadened the Liberals' base of support and, at one stage or another, played a decisive role in politics, although 1880 was not a time for them to do so. After the election the two representatives of the Right would have found it hard to join a government committed to extending the county franchise by placing it on the same basis as the borough franchise, so Goschen went as Special Ambassador to Constantinople and Lowe went to the House of Lords. Bright was probably the most active among these five leaders of the second rank: he had shaken

[1] For Hartington, *Manchester Guardian*, 26 Mar. and 2 Apr.; for Cross, ibid., 29 Mar.

[2] *The Times*, 24 Mar.; *East Suffolk Gazette*, 15 Apr.; Beaconsfield to Lady Bradford, 29 Mar.: Disraeli, *Letters to two Noble Ladies* (London, 1929), ii. 264.

off the illness, increased by irritation at ministerial office-work, that had affected him in 1874 and for some time after, and he strongly supported Gladstone's foreign policy. But he had very little to offer for the future apart from a warning to the Licensed Victuallers not to be too irreconcilably Conservative.[1] Chamberlain might have been expected to add something more constructive, but in fact he said very little during the election and concentrated on the organizational work of the National Liberal Federation.

The Conservatives had very few speakers to pit against these men. Smith in Westminster was well placed to attract attention, but the easy nature and general friendliness that made him popular in the Commons were not the qualities to catch the public attention during an election. He did not spend much time on party organization, though his work in his own constituency suggests that he could have made a useful contribution. Lord John Manners was in the Cabinet for his family name and Beaconsfield's memories of Young England, and Colonel Stanley had been slipped into the Cabinet to minimize the loss of Conservative influence in Lancashire at the time of Derby's resignation. Two men who were about to make their mark, Balfour and Lord Randolph Churchill, had sat for family boroughs during the 1874 Parliament without doing much to attract attention, and they played no conspicuous part in the election. None of the men elected for the first time in 1880, nor of the unsuccessful candidates, went on to outstanding careers— Walter Long, who was a candidate for the leadership of his party in 1911, perhaps went furthest. The Liberals had some interesting candidates in London: Bryce was elected, Morley was defeated, and Herbert Gladstone was defeated in Middlesex but was almost immediately afterwards elected to fill the seat kept for his father in Leeds. The most interesting newcomer to politics was affected by the rules against speeches by peers: the Midlothian campaigns introduced Lord Rosebery to political life.

It can be seen that, in the terms we should use to judge talent at present, the Liberals had the more powerful team

---

[1] G. M. Trevelyan, *Life of John Bright* (London, 1913), pp. 404–28; *The Times*, 20 and 22 Mar.

in the election. This was to some extent the natural result of the sort of candidates the two parties encouraged. Liberals had more often had to make their own way in the world or work in fairly competitive professions, and Conservatives were often decent steady landlords who had not had to exercise their talents.[1] The values of 1880 were a little different from ours, and established wealth and position were popular in the constituencies, especially in the counties.

Candidates had to be able to look after themselves during the three or four weeks of the election, for they got no help from central office to speak of. The machinery of the central offices began to run down because the organizers had to go away and fight their own electoral battles, and nobody seems to have found much use for a central organization that went on functioning while the constituency struggle was being fought. The value of a central office would have depended quite a lot on whether it knew what was going on in the election as a whole; so far as can be seen the Liberals, or at least Gladstone and Adam, had a fairly good idea of the situation and the Conservatives did not. To judge by his comments a day or two before the first results were known, Beaconsfield had no idea what was about to happen to his party,[2] and so it is unlikely that the Conservative central organization could have achieved very much even if it had continued to issue advice to candidates. Conservative candidates assumed that everything was going well, that everybody liked them and that no reasonable man could find anything convincing in the Liberal case.[3]

There is something a little strange in the way that the candidates could go on speaking to audiences without gathering what the result was going to be, though it is true that the swing of votes was, as usual, not very great.[4] But the London press encouraged the optimism of the Conservatives, and although the provincial press asserted after the election that it had done a great deal to influence the result, few provincial

[1] J. A. Thomas, *The House of Commons, 1832–1901* (London, 1939), pp. 14–16.
[2] See letter of Beaconsfield quoted on p. 30, n. 2.
[3] For examples, see the *Standard*, 23 Mar.
[4] To judge from figures in certain comparable constituencies printed in Hanham, op. cit., pp. 192–5, the swing to the Liberals was slightly larger in 1880 than the swing to the Conservatives in 1874. Also see below, pp. 134–5.

papers had predicted a great Liberal triumph.[1] This wide-spread failure to understand what was happening makes it uncertain how much real contact there was between the candidates and the voters. Gladstone did have some idea of the direction in which opinion was moving, and so it seems that he was more likely than other politicians to know what issues were considered important by the electorate.

The confidence of the Conservatives wilted with the first results, and they continued to lose seats steadily as the election went on. There is a slight indication that they lost seats at a greater rate in the later days of the election, but it was not an important factor: in the first four days 199 Conservative seats were contested, and the net Conservative loss was 58; in the rest of the election a further 149 Conservative seats were contested and the net loss was 51. The Conservatives had fallen from 348 to 239; the Liberals had risen from 243 to 351 and Home Rule had advanced from 57 to 62.[2]

The question of the Premiership arose at once and raised the issue of what had been at stake in the election. Gladstone's return to power would confirm his view of what the election had really decided. Beaconsfield had been confident enough of success to allow the Queen to leave for a holiday in Baden, from which she did not return until 17 April. Gladstone was determined to avoid demonstrations in favour of himself: he left Dalmeny for Hawarden very quietly on 6 April once the Midlothian result was known, and he rejected Plimsoll's idea of a triumphal reception in London with the comment that he was not going to take part in any sort of rejoicing over a fallen foe. This avoided the strain on Liberal unity that would have followed a suggestion that Gladstone was the leader responsible for the victory.[3]

This concern for party unity did not mean that he felt an obligation to serve under Granville or Hartington. The *Spectator* pointed out that even if Gladstone was not formally

---

[1] 'The New Parliament', *Edinburgh Review*, Apr. 1880, mentioned the *Scotsman*, the *Manchester Guardian*, and the *Leeds Mercury*.

[2] *The Times* gave running totals day by day.

[3] Morley, op. cit. ii. 168; draft of Gladstone to Plimsoll, 11 Apr.: Add. MSS. 44463, ff. 107–8; Gladstone's memorandum of 24 Apr.: Add. MSS. 44764, f. 55.

at the head of a Liberal government he would command the allegiance of so many of its members that he would have effective power.[1] Ex-Premiers did not often accept subordinate office; Lord John Russell had served under Aberdeen in a coalition and under Palmerston, but Palmerston had established much stronger claims to supremacy than either Granville or Hartington. Fairly clearly it was the Queen's duty to send for one or other of the official leaders so that the position could be made explicit, but the Queen did not like the idea of Gladstone returning as Prime Minister, and Beaconsfield seems to have thought that this result could be avoided.[2] Even after he had found the official leaders unable to form a government, he wrote to the Queen in terms that suggested it was their duty to form one and that they had to take the responsibility of advising that Gladstone be made Prime Minister.[3] Beaconsfield greatly overestimated the amount of support that Hartington possessed, and suggested that he could form a government. On party grounds, a Hartington ministry had the advantage, from the Conservative point of view, that if a moderate Liberal was installed as Prime Minister, the advanced Liberals might be so disappointed that they would attack him and drive him into the arms of the Tories: Beaconsfield may have seen Hartington as a second Palmerston, defended from the Radicals by the Conservatives. On policy grounds, Beaconsfield would naturally prefer a Liberal who had shown some restraint in condemning his conduct of foreign affairs.

Beaconsfield seems to have been acting in perfectly good faith when he told the Queen that there were 237 Whigs (i.e. supporters of Hartington) in the Commons, for he gave the same figures to Northcote.[4] However, the figures were wrong, and sufficiently wrong to make it quite understandable that Herbert Gladstone, commenting many years later on Beaconsfield's advice, should suspect that there had been

[1] Gladstone's memorandum of 23 Apr.: Add. MSS. 44764, f. 44. *Spectator*, 17 Apr.

[2] The Queen's memorandum of 18 Apr., and Beaconsfield to the Queen, 21 Apr: Monypenny and Buckle, op. cit. vi. 535–6.

[3] Beaconsfield to the Queen, 23 Apr.: ibid., p. 538.

[4] Beaconsfield to the Queen, 21 Apr.: ibid., p. 536; Andrew Lang, *Life of Sir Stafford Northcote* (Edinburgh, 1890), ii. 149.

a deliberate attempt to use the Queen to cause dissension among the Liberals. Herbert Gladstone's own estimate that 70 of the Liberal M.P.s were Chamberlainite and 70 Hartingtonian, with the broad central majority Gladstonian, seems roughly accurate.[1] Even in Gladstone's absence, Hartington would have faced difficulties: Wolverton estimated that the men above and below the gangway were likely to balance.[2] Apart from the feeling of the Members, there was a certain amount of outside pressure: at meetings there were shouts from the crowd that Gladstone should take the lead, and a group of prominent Liberals passed a motion thanking Hartington and Granville for their services but declaring that Gladstone should become Prime Minister. The newspapers said he should form the government, though on the Conservative side this view may have been tinged with the malicious thought that it would cause trouble for the Liberals.[3]

Confronted by this heavy parliamentary and extra-parliamentary pressure, Granville and Hartington would have found it very hard to resist Gladstone's claims to power. Granville, the leader of the party, had no desire to do so: he liked, respected, admired, and often understood Gladstone, and had felt for some time that at an opportune moment he should resume the leadership. The effective leader of the opposition, he had always felt, was the man who showed the party most sport, and there was no doubt in his mind that Gladstone had led in the pursuit of Beaconsfield.[4] Even if he had not been personally a strong Gladstonian, the difficulty of controlling the large and exuberant Liberal majority in the Commons from the House of Lords might well have discouraged him from attempting to form a government.

Hartington was in a different position. He had grown in authority during his five years as leader of the Liberals in the Commons and he had played a prominent part in the campaign. Furthermore he did not like or trust Gladstone.

[1] Herbert Gladstone, op. cit., pp. 356–9 and 177–8.
[2] Wolverton to Gladstone, 6 Apr.: Add. MSS. 44349, ff. 126–9.
[3] Henry Gladstone's account in F. W. Hirst, *Gladstone as Financier and Economist* (London, 1931), p. 314; Bristol Liberal meeting and Hackney Liberal meeting, *Daily News*, 17 and 22 Apr.; *Pall Mall Gazette*, 23 Apr.
[4] Granville to Gladstone, 27 May 1877: Add. MSS. 44171, ff. 79–80.

If he had obeyed his inclination he would have withdrawn from an ostensible leadership which had now become a mockery; but he was advised that any such action on his part would split the party, and he doggedly held on till after the dissolution [*sic*] of March 1880. People praised his loyalty to Gladstone but he said to me in later days 'I thought that Gladstone had not behaved well to me, and I did not feel the least loyalty to him. That is quite the wrong word.'

He found it hard to understand Gladstone, and towards the end of their association he gave up the attempt to do so. It is possible that their disagreements began when Gladstone tried to send Hartington to Dublin as Lord Lieutenant in 1868 and Hartington forced his way into the Cabinet instead. Harcourt encouraged Hartington to assert himself in 1880 and attempt to form a government; it can be seen that Hartington would have had no moral objection to doing so, but his natural indolence may have reinforced his estimate that it was not possible for him to do so.[1]

When the Queen had got back from Germany and had consulted Beaconsfield, she sent for Hartington. A modern constitutional theorist might have preferred her to call on the party leader, Lord Granville, and it will be noted that Beaconsfield's advice was not binding—in short, sending for Hartington made it clear to politicians that she wanted to keep Gladstone out. When Hartington came, on 22 April, he explained that he could neither persuade Gladstone to enter his government nor form a government without Gladstone. Next day the Queen saw Granville and Hartington together and found the situation unchanged, and on 24 April she accepted the inevitable and asked Gladstone to form a government. Her line of conduct may have been constitutionally correct, but the conduct of policy was likely to suffer because of her evident dislike for the eventual result.

Gladstone's position as Prime Minister may have been strengthened by the demonstration that he was the only person who could form a government. If the Queen had given way at once to what was fairly clearly the people's choice, Hartington or even Granville would still have remained possible centres for moderate Liberal sentiment. As

[1] G. W. E. Russell, *Portraits of the Seventies* (London, 1916), p. 92; B. Holland, *Life of the Eighth Duke of Devonshire* (London, 1911), i. 73 and 288.

it was, the weakness of their position had been demonstrated, and the Queen herself was in a less good position to restrain Gladstone in his choice of ministers. Not that much restraint was necessary; Gladstone wanted to form his Cabinet on conventional lines, giving no places to people who had not first held junior office, which would have excluded Chamberlain. Eventually Gladstone was obliged to take him in, but the basically non-Radical nature of the Cabinet had been indicated. It has been suggested by Mr. Shannon that the non-Radical approach meant that the Liberal party was drawn away from its manifest destiny, but that lies outside the scope of this book.[1]

[1] R. T. Shannon, op. cit., pp. 272–4.

II

THE ISSUES IN DISPUTE

THE best summary of the issues in the campaign is the *Punch* cartoon of the Colossus of Words. A full-length, full-page drawing of Gladstone shows him standing with one foot on the quay of Peace and the other on the quay of Retrenchment, while the ship Reform sails between them into harbour. In one hand he holds the beacon-light Finance, in the other the beacon-light Foreign Affairs.[1]

Inevitably the cartoon cannot fully express the extent to which these issues were presented in moral terms. The unifying thread of the Midlothian speeches was an indictment against the government, which was charged with diplomatic and financial incompetence and wickedness. Gladstone said that the election should be treated as a sort of state trial,[2] in which the electorate was to be a jury either condemning government policy or approving it and taking the responsibility for it. The Liberal party, as prosecuting counsel, was to go over the past record of the government, concentrating on finance and foreign policy, and from this examination it would emerge whether the Conservatives were fit to go on ruling or should be replaced. The implication, nowhere very clearly stated, was that future prospects and promises mattered very little, and that greater attention than usual should be paid to questions involving the government's fidelity to moral principle.

Gladstone was very successful in imposing this pattern on the election.[3] The importance of moral principles, and the need to apply them to government policy, was accepted. Candidates chose to speak about finance and foreign policy, and when they discussed foreign policy they usually argued about past events. This was not at all what Beaconsfield had

---

[1] *Punch*, 13 Dec. 1879.

[2] Speech of 2 Apr., *Speeches in Scotland*, ii. 78.

[3] Speech of Bright, *The Times*, 29 Mar. *The Times*, 13 Apr., declared that the verdict had been a calm one.

wanted: in the letter that he wrote to the Duke of Marlborough, as an election manifesto, he put forward the threat
of Home Rule agitation and the need for Britain to maintain
her 'ascendancy' in Europe to keep the peace as the subjects
for discussion in the election. But important though these
subjects were, nobody was interested.

People found it hard to be concerned about Ireland because it was still politically tranquil at the time of the election, and because there was apparently no difference of
opinion to be discussed. Ireland had suffered badly from the
agricultural failure of 1879, a Bill to provide cheap money
for relief works was passed during the short session of 1880,
and two rival Relief Funds, under the Duchess of Marlborough and the Lord Mayor of Dublin, had been set
up, but outrages attracted no attention. Nobody seriously
believed that the Liberal party supported Home Rule, and
this deprived Beaconsfield's attack of much of its relevance.

Irish affairs might have been brought up more effectively
if Parnell had been in the country at the time of the dissolution. He was in America, collecting funds for Irish famine
relief and the Irish political organizations, but returned
quickly to Ireland and devoted himself to making sure that
resolute and determined men were selected as candidates.[1]
The discussion in Ireland turned on Home Rule and the
possibility of altering the land law,[2] but despite the rapidly
worsening agricultural situation there was no sign of a great
swing of opinion to Home Rule. The Home Rule vote
increased, but the total vote cast in Ireland increased at very
nearly the same rate. Home Rule gained a few seats, but
1880 cannot rank with 1874 and 1885 as a year of great
electoral upheaval in Ireland. The struggle for power within
the Home Rule party may have reduced its electoral effectiveness, and Parnell's insistence on discipline may have
increased its parliamentary efficiency, but it is quite understandable that the election did nothing to make English
leaders take Home Rule more seriously.

Lord Hartington was perhaps the most outspoken in

---

[1] C. C. O'Brien, *Parnell and his Party* (London, 1957), pp. 23–27; *Morning Post*, 22 Mar.
[2] Ibid., 31 Mar.

repudiating Home Rule. It is true that at the time of the
Liverpool by-election he declined to exclude the Liberal
candidate from the party although Lord Ramsay had, while
fishing for Irish votes, committed himself to voting for an
inquiry into steps for granting Home Rule; but he made it
clear that, as party leader, he would accept no change in the
constitutional relationship between England and Ireland.[1]
As was to be expected, Gladstone was more imaginative and
less unequivocal: he said that the real threat to the Union
came from the Conservatives who had imposed an alien
Church and an alien land system on the Irish, and had fixed
a higher voting qualification for Irish electors although their
country was poorer than England. The fact that only £4
householders could vote was an illustration of the inequality
of the relationship, and Liberals could show their pro-Irish
feeling without committing themselves to Home Rule by
asking for uniformity in the franchise.[2]

At a more personal level Conservatives condemned the
attitude of Lord Ramsay and Liberals pointed to Colonel
King-Harman, an Irish landlord who was Lord-Lieutenant
of his county and stood, unsuccessfully, as a Conservative
candidate, but had said he was in favour of Home Rule.[3]
One of the few Liberals to declare their approval of Home
Rule was Joseph Cowen, the Radical Member from Newcastle. Neither side knew what to do about this, for Cowen
shared the Home Rule party approval of Beaconsfield's
foreign policy, which made him a favourite of the Conservatives and an embarrassment to the Liberals.[4]

While Beaconsfield's election letter was important because
it helped guide Irish voters into the Liberal camp, the
phrases in it which meant most to the majority of voters in
Great Britain were the references to the ascendancy of Eng-

[1] *The Times,* 10 Feb. and 19 Mar.

[2] Ibid., 22 Mar. See also addresses of Rogers, Agnew, and Herbert Gladstone,
ibid., 15, 18, and 20 Mar.

[3] It was said that Ulster Conservatives had at first supported Home Rule:
Sullivan's speech, *Manchester Guardian,* 2 Feb. On King-Harman, speeches of
Harcourt, Hartington, and Gladstone, *The Times,* 4 Feb., 15 and 22 Mar.

[4] In Hereford Clive said that, though a Liberal, he approved of the government's
foreign policy, and he said that he stood with Cowen. He was asked if he was a
Radical and a Home Ruler and replied that he did not know about this aspect of
Cowen's opinions. *Hereford Times,* 14 and 21 Feb.

land in Europe. To some extent foreign policy from 1876 to 1878 became the central issue because it was an area of common ground on which the parties wanted to fight,[1] and they confined themselves to arguing about the past because neither party had a policy for the future that would stand discussion. In any case the issues at stake in the Eastern crisis of 1876–8, and in the Zulu and Afghan Wars, were quite fundamental enough to provide material for arguing about which party should govern.

If moderate men like Hartington or Northcote or Derby had been in charge of policy they might have found a bi-partisan approach to the Eastern crisis which avoided the risks of enthusiastic single-handed support for Turkey and the dangers of strengthening Russia too much. Gladstone and Beaconsfield represented the most thoroughly com-mitted wings of their parties,[2] and they found their position helped by the changes in party organization. Large numbers of voluntary workers were needed, and would almost cer-tainly come from the ranks of the people most interested in politics. No doubt the bulk of the voters in 1880 were con-cerned with simple domestic questions concerned with the cost of living and the level of unemployment,[3] but they were brought to vote by men who were concerned about foreign policy, and Gladstone and Beaconsfield owed their dominant position in their parties at the time to their ability to arouse enthusiasm on this subject.

The Liberal policy in the Eastern crisis had been that England should work with the other Powers to maintain the harmony of the Concert of Europe. The Turkish govern-ment should be kept under control, prevented from mas-sacring its Christian subjects and induced to give up some of its territory in Europe. There was disagreement in the party about how far England should go in support of this

[1] Harcourt in 'Speeches by Liberals in the Recess', B.M. 8139 6 6(12); speeches by King's Lynn and Mid-Kent Conservatives, *Morning Post*, 11 and 12 Mar.; editorials, ibid., 19, 20, 22, and 23 Mar., *Daily News*, 6 Feb., 25 Mar., 10 Apr.

[2] R. W. Seton-Watson, *Gladstone, Disraeli and the Eastern Question* (London, 1935), p. 561.

[3] There is a letter by a Liberal M.P. to this effect in the *Daily News*, 23 Feb. At one point Gladstone received a working men's address: he underlined the para-graph about foreign affairs but did not mark the paragraph about the depression: Add. MSS. 44666, f. 102.

policy, and the party leaders moved away from Gladstone
when he seemed to be considering, after the breakdown of
the Concert at the end of 1876, a policy of co-operating with
Russia to impose demands on Turkey by force. However,
once Russia had declared war on Turkey, early in 1877,
Liberal efforts were confined to keeping England from
entering the war on Turkey's side.

Conservative policy had initially been to maintain Turkey's territorial integrity and independence from external
interference or supervision, an approach with obvious Palmerstonian foundations, and while this policy had to be replaced
by one of partition, the Conservatives felt they were basing
themselves firmly on the policy upheld in the Crimean War.
But by the 1870s the old Palmerstonian certainties had faded
a little, and the ideals of a moral foreign policy held by
Gladstone's old leader Aberdeen were more widespread.
Emphasis on the maintenance of the interests of England
had become something of a characteristically Conservative
attitude; many Liberals accepted the internationalist ideals
expounded in Gladstone's West Calder speech of 27 November 1879, in which he said that foreign policy should be
based on fostering the strength of the empire, preserving
the peace, maintaining the Concert of Europe, avoiding need-
less and entangling alliances, acknowledging the equal rights
of all nations, and should be inspired by a love of freedom.[1]

The Conservatives were not particularly concerned to
argue about the merits of their pro-Turkish position; taking
this for granted they concentrated on the skill and determination with which the policy had been carried out without
going to war, and they pointed out that Liberal indecisive-
ness had had a lot to do with the outbreak of the Crimean
War. Liberal speakers also referred to events of an equally
distant past, such as the Repeal of the Corn Laws and the
ending of the Paper Duties. These excursions into ancient
history would seem out of place in a mid-twentieth-century
election; perhaps in 1880 they had the same effect as singing
'The Red Flag' or 'Land of Hope and Glory' would have
at the present day.

The Conservatives clearly considered that their foreign

---

[1] *Speeches in Scotland*, i. 58–66.

policy had been very popular at the moment of crisis, and they referred to the way that it had been supported in Parliament by majorities larger than the fifty—over Liberals and Home Rulers together—that they gained in the 1874 election. These large majorities had been gained sometimes because the Liberal leaders thought their most active followers were heading for war against Turkey, and sometimes because a large number of Home Rulers and half a dozen Liberals preferred the government's policy to Gladstone's or Hartington's, but neither sort of support was very relevant during the campaign.

By 1880 Liberals were prepared to accept the Treaty, on the grounds of continuity of foreign policy, but this did not mean they accepted the policy underlying it. Even if it had been popular in 1878, Beaconsfield himself had admitted in 1876 that it was not favoured by the majority of the country, and the Liberals hoped to reawaken this feeling. They objected both to the purpose of Conservative policy and to the way it had been carried out; by the time of the election they were concentrating on the latter point, partly because it raised an issue of general application and partly because it was less likely to divide their own party. The break-up of the Concert of Europe, the willingness to run the danger of war, and the use of surprising strokes of policy and secret diplomacy were all condemned. By concentrating on the way policy had been carried out they made the issue into a test of character.[1]

Beaconsfield's phrase 'Peace with Honour' was not taken up and repeated by Conservative candidates, nor was his dismissal of the reports of the 1876 massacres as 'coffee-house babble' taken up by the Liberals. However, they did stress the charge that the pro-Turkish policy had been pursued by underhand means. Six occasions were listed on which the government had deceived the public or, to use politer language, had produced great 'surprises' during the Eastern crisis, and there was a suggestion that the unexpected dissolution was itself another surprise. The government had not conducted its policy by discussion in an open

---

[1] Gladstone's speech, 17 Mar., ibid. ii. 17; *Daily News*, 27 Mar.; speeches of Cross and Hartington, *The Times*, 19 and 26 Mar.

Congress of the Powers but by secret preliminary agreements with Russia and Turkey; when Marvin the clerk who copied them out had given their contents to *The Globe* Lord Salisbury prevaricated by calling them 'unauthentic' though they were fundamental to British diplomacy at the Congress of Berlin.[1]

There were of course also objections to the substance of Conservative policy; it was too obviously based on power politics, it had not prevented the outbreak of the Russo-Turkish War, it had handed Christians back to Moslem rule, and it had broken up the Concert of Europe. But the Conservatives had replies for these charges, asserting that they had kept the Russians out of Constantinople, had not involved England in war, and yet had made her more respected among the nations than she had been since the death of Palmerston. The charges left unanswered were those directed against underhand dealing; it is not clear what the electorate thought about it, but at least the government's honesty was a relevant topic.[2]

The Conservative complaints that Liberals were trimming their principles for election-time were probably inaccurate, but they show confidence that foreign policy was an advantageous election issue and that a return to the spirit of 1878 was the way to victory. The government claimed that everyone in Europe, except of course the Russians, hoped for a Conservative victory and that the only thing which could draw together all continental opinion was a desire for peace: a firm and decisive British government, which made its intentions clear, was the best guarantee of peace. This may have been a fair comment on the way Lord Salisbury produced a more decisive policy than Lord Derby, but the country had been close enough to war in 1878 for this preservation-of-peace argument to seem unconvincing. In any case there was something close to a contradiction between

---

[1] Hartington on the infrequent use of the slogan, *The Times*, 15 Mar.; Gladstone's speech of 18 Nov. 1879, *Speeches in Scotland*, i. 18; speeches of Hartington, *Manchester Guardian*, 30 Mar., 2 and 5 Apr.; 'The New Parliament', *Edinburgh Review*, Apr. 1880.

[2] Speeches of Gladstone, Lowther, and Cross, *The Times*, 18, 20, and 22 Mar.; Hartington pointed out that Palmerston had given up the Ionian Islands, ibid., 2 Apr.

Beaconsfield's statement that Europe was so disturbed that a Conservative government was necessary and Northcote's statement that the Conservative government had made Europe tranquil. However, both arguments did have the attraction of reminding people that Britain was very important in a sense she had not been in 1874.[1]

The Liberals replied that it was not the business of British statesmen to make themselves popular in Europe. When Gladstone said the Emperor of Austria was reported to hope for a Conservative victory and went on to ask where on the map anybody could say, 'Here Austria did good', he upset the diplomats, but he also combined British patriotism and British morality against the party the Austrians wanted to be successful. It was not possible for the Liberals to equal their opponents in appealing to the patriotic emotions, but it was relatively easy for them to argue that they were not traitors, and that they were more moral and upright than the Conservatives.[2]

The acquisition of Cyprus was not stressed by Conservatives; the Liberals attacked it on the grounds that Cyprus was no use because it had no good harbour, and that it had been acquired in an immoral way. The aquisition of territory linked foreign policy and colonial questions, and this was probably a disadvantage for the government. Attacks on Little Englandism were made much less convincing by the failure of expansionist ventures in the colonies. The massacre of the envoy to Afghanistan and his entourage, and the subsequent Afghan revolt which looked as though it might receive Russian help, could only harm the government. The occupation of the Transvaal aroused little interest during the election, but there was little to be said to defend the early disasters of Sir Bartle Frere's preventive war against the Zulus; the government had censured him in terms that would have made much more sense if he had been recalled.

---

[1] Speeches of Lord George Hamilton, *The Times*, 17 Mar.; of Hicks Beach, ibid., 25 Mar.; of Cross, ibid., 26 and 29 Mar.; of the French press, ibid., 27 Mar.

[2] Gladstone on Austria, *Speeches in Scotland*, ii. 14; on charges of being a Russian agent, ibid. i. 60; later he quoted Russell's remark in the Don Pacifico debate that Palmerston 'had not been the foreign minister of Austria or of Russia or of any other state; he had been the foreign minister of England', ibid. ii. 77. See also speeches of Forster, Cohen, and James, *The Times*, 22 and 40 Mar.

There was very little in all this to which the Conservatives could refer with pride. On the other hand, Liberal references to the government's failure could look very like rejoicing over British defeats; it was probably safer to leave Isandhlwana and the death of the Prince Imperial to speak for themselves, while pointing out the weaknesses of the government's Afghan policy. The Viceroy's Instructions on Afghanistan had been drawn up by Lord Salisbury, whom very few Liberals felt able to trust by 1880; they seemed calculated to drive the Emir to despair or into the arms of Russia. Lord Roberts had alienated the press by his treatment of correspondents during the campaign, and the Viceroy had also alarmed it by his attitude to the Indian vernacular press. The plight of the Afghan families driven out into the winter snow by the invading army led Gladstone to make a great appeal to the internationalism and the humanity of his listeners. The Conservatives argued that the Liberal policy of refusing an alliance in the early 70s when the Emir asked for it was responsible for the trouble. The Liberal reply was that the Emir had wanted too much because he had asked for a guarantee of support in case of internal revolt. It seems unlikely that audiences were interested either by this or by the initial Conservative charge.[1]

On the whole the 'prancing preconsuls'[2] probably served to reduce people's enthusiasm for an exciting foreign policy and to weaken the desire for imperial expansion. The idea of expanding and asserting British power which underlay Beaconsfield's attitude to the Eastern Question also inspired the policy of activity on the frontiers of the empire, and the Liberal attack was launched against the whole external policy of the government. Beaconsfield's policy was not an amoral one which relied on success for its justification, but it was unlikely to arouse enthusiasm unless it was successful.

[1] On Cyprus, speech of Goschen, *Morning Post*, 16 Mar.; speeches of Cross, *The Times*, 22 and 26 Mar.; speeches of Hartington, ibid., 23 and 30 Mar. On Africa, speeches of Hartington and Hicks-Beach, ibid., 25 Mar. Gladstone in his first Midlothian campaign stressed Afghanistan more than Zululand, *Speeches in Scotland*, i. 46–47. Speeches of Lord George Hamilton, the Solicitor-General and Forster, *The Times*, 22 Mar.; Lowe, ibid., 25 Mar.; Cross, ibid., 26 Mar.; and Hartington, ibid., 30 Mar.

[2] Harcourt's speech of 11 Apr. 1879: *The Times*, 12 Apr.

Nobody had been excited, though they might be satisfied, by the moral justifications provided, so all the emotional foundations of the policy were removed when people lost interest in continental supremacy. The Liberals argued that the Conservative attitude to the Eastern Question was one which sooner or later led to disaster, and that the electorate had to pass judgement on it. The politicians disregarded, almost unanimously, the pronouncement of *The Times*: 'The great foreign questions which divided parties during the last three years are for the time closed, as far as Parliamentary discussion is concerned. We are entering a new phase of foreign and colonial affairs, and the interval is necessarily calm.' A new period was at hand, but it could begin only after the election.[1]

Perhaps because they relied heavily on the popularity of their foreign policy the Conservatives did not try to turn to the subject of the social legislation passed by Beaconsfield's government in its early years. This legislation has received enough attention from subsequent writers to make necessary an explanation for its failure to appear in the election. The remark attributed to Alexander Macdonald that the Conservatives 'have done more for the working man in five years than the Liberals did in fifty' has been quoted so often that people could be excused for thinking it was an important issue in the campaign and that Macdonald joined the Conservatives.[2]

So far as can be seen Macdonald shared the general belief that legislating for the working man was not the primary purpose of Parliament. At any rate, he remained a Liberal and there is no sign that he would have had many followers if he had left his party. The Conservatives, for their part, did not share Beaconsfield's belief in the Conservative working man and were quite ready to say nothing about the

---

[1] The *Spectator* had said, 'the new electors greatly enjoy seeing fireworks', but might quickly lose interest in the Treaty of Berlin, 6 July 1878; the *Standard* said the election was simply a question of whether Britain was to be great, 9 Mar. 1880. *The Times*, 26 Mar.

[2] Monypenny and Buckle, op. cit. v. 369, gives this epigrammatic quotation without a reference. *The Times*, 15 Jan. 1879, reported Macdonald said, 'they had had enough of Whig rule. When [? since] he entered Parliament they had gained more from the Conservatives in respect of matters affecting the working-man than the Liberals would ever have granted.'

subject. They had no proposals for further government action to help the working class, and their references to Beaconsfield's efforts in the past were extremely perfunctory. Beaconsfield's own manifesto did not mention the past legislation nor did it make any references to the future. Conservatives spoke of codifying the Criminal Law and revising the Patent Law and the Bankruptcy Law. No doubt these would have been very useful steps to take, but they were not novel, they were not distinctively Conservative, and while they might help businessmen they did nothing for working men. If an enfranchised working man wanted a politician who spoke in terms of helping the working classes he had to turn to Chamberlain or Bradlaugh, though neither of them put forward specific legislation that was likely to be very helpful.[1]

When references were made to Beaconsfield's legislation by Conservatives who felt it would attract some support, their speeches were very vague, and did not pick out any particular Act for commendation. All the social legislation produced had been passed in the 1875 Session, and the fact that it could be passed quickly was a sign that it was not very controversial.[2] Trade Unions found it was easier to conduct a strike legally, but this was a relatively small advantage at a time of depression. Borough councils could build houses, but only if they exercised the powers given to them. Tenants could expect compensation for the improvements they made on the land they rented, but the landlord could reserve this power by specific words, and usually made use of his right. Legislation of this sort was described reasonably enough as 'not law-making but leave-taking'.[3] The Public Health Act did little more than consolidate previous Acts and make their

[1] 'The Tory View of Lord Beaconsfield', *Contemporary Review*, Dec. 1879; address of Lord John Manners, *The Times*, 16 Mar.; City Conservatives, *Morning Post*, 19 Mar., speech of Northcote, *The Times*, 26 Mar. The *Daily News*, 22 Mar., inquired what all this legislation was to be.

[2] Bagehot had a low opinion of Disraeli's capacity for everyday parliamentary business. 'In 1867 he made a minority achieve wonderful things; but in 1876, when he had the best majority—the most numerous and obedient—since Mr. Pitt, he did nothing with it. So far from being able to pass great enactments, he could not even despatch ordinary business at decent hours', W. Bagehot, *Historical Essays* (London, 1965), p. 294.

[3] H. W. Lucy, *The Disraeli Parliament* (London, 1884), p. 101.

application more widespread. In short, while the principle behind this interventionist legislation was important, though less novel than Dicey—to take a very eminent example—supposed, it made little change in men's lives at the time.

Because their scope appeared wider than it was, the Liberals could argue that the Conservative legislation gave with one hand and took away with the other, and thus they implied that nothing at all had been achieved.[1] Some Conservatives claimed that they could have produced more legislation if it had not been for Obstruction, but they gave no hint what this legislation would have been, and Obstruction was principally used as an issue to consolidate anti-Irish feeling. The Conservatives still claimed to take an interest in the working man, and supporters of Tory Democracy still hoped to unite the upper and the lower classes against the middle class, but it was very difficult to suggest any legislation that could have this effect. Substantial help for the working class meant heavy taxes for the rich, assistance for tenant farmers meant attacking the privileges of the landlord. A policy of nationalism, involving the threat of war, might attract the upper and lower classes more than the middle, but there is no sign that Beaconsfield thought of his foreign policy as a substitute for Tory Democracy.[2]

Protection, or Fair Trade as it was known at the time, was not a serious issue. Salisbury hinted at it in his Manchester speech of October 1879, but it aroused no response. Ecroyd, from Lancashire, who had put forward the case for Protection for industry, stood on a Free Trade platform, and Chaplin in Lincolnshire, who was regarded as the champion of agricultural Protection, avoided the issue. Agricultural and industrial Protection were never presented as a coherent programme, and supporters of one aspect of Protection were quite likely to feel that the other aspect was undesirable. Subsequent history suggests that a time of depression is tactically suitable for launching a Protectionist campaign, but flirting with Protection in 1879 and saying nothing

---

[1] Address of the Liberal candidates for Hastings, *The Times*, 18 Mar. See also *Daily News*, 19 Mar.

[2] Speeches of Smith, Cross, and Sandon, *The Times*, 20, 25, and 30 Mar.; 'How shall I vote: a question for working-men', Conservative Central Office pamphlets.

about it in 1880 merely gave the Liberals an attractive and defenceless target to shoot at.[1]

Fourteen Liberal candidates in the election approved of the government's foreign policy. They did badly; none of the four newcomers were successful, two other prospective candidates had to withdraw, two of the ten sitting Members were displaced by other Liberals, and of the eight survivors, Beaumont had to move from South Durham to South Northumberland and Walter had to depend on Conservative votes. Nevertheless they were important enough to use as an indication that the Liberals were disunited and unfit for office.[2]

Probably they were not more disunited than they had been under Russell and Palmerston, though the threat to Hartington's position revealed by Gladstone's return to politics was serious enough to indicate the lines along which the party would divide if a crisis occurred. The appeals for unity in the ranks, and the efforts to prevent rival Liberal candidates from appearing, were attacked by the Conservatives as a dishonest policy designed to win power for an uneasy coalition with no common principles except a desire for the spoils of office.[3] Gladstone's Resolutions of May 1877 might have divided the party along lines that went even deeper than foreign policy. The Whigs and moderate Liberals, who would not have supported the original five resolutions, were not fiery reformers by temperament or by interest, and could not be driven too hard. The Conservatives exaggerated Liberal divisions, before and after the election: Gladstone withdrew all but one of his resolutions in 1877, and at the time of the election *The Economist* said:

The most Radical measures that a Liberal government is likely to bring forward are an assimilation of the county franchise to the franchise which the Conservatives themselves deliberately adopted for boroughs, and an abolition of the conveyancing differences that now exist between the descent of real and other property.[4]

[1] *Annual Register for 1879*, p. 81; speeches of Hartington, *The Times*, 24 and 25 Mar.; a big and a small, pre-1846 loaf were produced at one of Hartington's meetings and also in Derbyshire, *Manchester Guardian*, 29 Mar. and *New Mills and Hayfield Advertiser*, 9 Apr.

[2] Speech of Sandon, *Morning Post*, 3 Feb.; speech of Cross, *The Times*, 1 Apr.

[3] 'Credentials of the Opposition', *Quarterly Review*, Jan. 1880; 'Brummagem Morality', *Blackwood's Magazine*, Apr. 1880.

[4] *The Economist*, 28 Mar.

The Radicals may have thought this was a first instalment, and some Whigs may have thought it a final instalment of reform, but it was a programme on which everybody could agree for the time being. Disestablishment might remain in the back of nonconformist minds, and supporters of Temperance legislation had not retired from the battle, but these dangerous issues which could destroy Liberal unity were kept out of sight. At the 1880 Conference of the National Liberal Federation Chamberlain said Radicals and moderates had to go some of the way together, and if they were fated to quarrel they should wait until the moment when parting became inevitable.[1] That moment was not 1880, for the good but unspoken reason that the Radicals could expect to benefit from the extension of the franchise. Supporters of the causes kept out of sight tended to rally round the Federation, and the Conservatives attacked the Caucus accordingly.

The American nickname 'Caucus' was certainly intended to suggest that the branches of the National Liberal Federation would import American practices like a partisan civil service, corruption in contracts, and rule by politicians who were not gentlemen. There was some justification for the latter charge, because the attraction of the National Liberal Federation lay in providing a way for the post-1867 electorate to take part in politics, and this was likely to weaken the position of the upper classes. Quite possibly weakening the upper classes was the highest unifying factor in the National Liberal Federation, but the first steps it wanted to take in this direction were unexceptionable.[2] Placing Radicals in the Cabinet, giving the vote to householders in the counties, limiting election expenses and redistributing seats were measures on which almost all Liberals could agree, and as they helped the Federation and the opposition to the upper classes which it represented Chamberlain had no need to make any overt demonstration against the leaders of his party; he could afford to wait until after the electoral system had been revised.

The Federation made its Radical views clear at its Conferences. It wanted Disestablishment, local option or the

---

[1] *The Times,* 4 Feb.
[2] J. Chamberlain, 'The Caucus', B.M. 8138 cc 8 (7).

Gothenburg system of municipal monopoly in drink, a Burials Bill to ease the position of nonconformists and legislation to deprive landlords of the privileges given them by the Game Laws and the Law of Settlement and Entail. These measures were not official party policy, and probably could never have been the policy of a party which contained a body of Whig noblemen, but the fact that they had an organization with these views kept the 'crochet-mongers' within the Liberal party.[1]

It also provided the Conservatives with a line of attack. Not only could they claim that the uneasy alliance of Liberals and Radicals would not survive for long, but also they could claim that the Radical tail would wag the Liberal dog. The electorate was told that if it voted Liberal it was giving power not to Hartington but to Gladstone, behind whom stood Chamberlain, behind whom stood Parnell.[2] Undoubtedly there were tensions beneath the surface unity of Liberal and Radical. They became clear for a few days in 1879 on the question of flogging in the army, when the Radicals under Chamberlain forced Hartington to lay aside his sympathy with the officers and declare himself against it. The issue of flogging was mentioned during the election, and it became clear that Hartington had chosen the popular side, but it was hardly a question that could break up the party.[3]

The Home Rule split in 1886 seems to give weight to the Tory statements, which were repeated even after the result, that the Liberal coalition was unlikely to survive. But the Conservatives would have had to admit that the Liberal party was still united in its desire for constitutional change, and the events of 1886 suggest that the only thing likely to divide the Liberals was a large measure of legislation on which a substantial body of Liberals could join the Conservatives without being accused of inconsistency. Ireland need not have been the issue; an attack on the Church or

[1] Reports of Conferences of the National Liberal Federation, 1–9.

[2] Speeches of Cross, Ritchie, Lord George Hamilton, Duncan, and Stanhope, *The Times*, 19, 20, 22, and 24 Mar., and 6 Apr.

[3] Anti-flogging posters from Oxford, Portsmouth, and Southwark, Nuffield Collection, folio vol. ii; *Daily News* report on Wilton, 20 Mar. (one of the very few constituency reports to appear); a letter in the *Hereford Times*, 17 Apr., said it was astonishing how much harm the question of flogging had done to the Conservatives.

the landlords, or an attempt to make the rich pay ransom, might have had the same effect.

The Eastern crisis might have caused serious problems of party unity in 1877 and 1878, but the division had been healed by 1880. Opposition to Beaconsfield's policy had inspired many party workers in the days when Gladstone stood alone as the representative of morality in high places. By the time of the election it was clear that forceful foreign policies sometimes led to failure, and Gladstone had modified his position to show that he was willing to accept existing treaty obligations. The Conservatives concentrated a good deal of their attention on Gladstone; the Liberals were equally ready to denounce Beaconsfield's moral obliquity but they did not dwell on the fact that he was older than Gladstone, nor did they suggest that his mental or physical powers were failing, although by this time he was physically much weaker than Gladstone. The attacks on Gladstone do not seem to have been well received, and their vehemence may have encouraged the advanced Liberals to accept him; he had no very striking Radical proposals to make, but the Radicals may well have loved him for the enemies he had made.

While the Liberals renounced Home Rule vehemently enough to prevent it from becoming an issue, the Conservatives tried to argue that the Liberals could not hope to get a majority which would be 'independent' of the Irish Members, though it was not clear whether this meant they would not do as well as in 1868, when the Liberals elected in Great Britain outnumbered the whole Conservative party, or that the Liberals could never stand against a combination of Conservatives and Home Rulers. In the event the argument may have recoiled, because after the first day's voting the Liberals could claim that the only way to avoid having a ministry dependent on Home Rulers was to make the Liberal majority overwhelming.[1]

This side issue about the probable state of the parties after the election was the nearest that people came to discussing the Irish Question. Despite the prescient words of Beaconsfield's election letter the topic was neglected; the Liberals

---

[1] Speeches by Cross and Northcote, *The Times*, 22 and 26 Mar.; for the Liberal replies, speeches of Hartington and Forster, ibid., 2 and 5 Apr.

saw no advantage in taking it up, and the Conservatives saw
no prospect of getting anyone to listen, so the problem was
almost entirely neglected in Great Britain. After the election
it meant that the Liberals had to face the question with no
mandate for drastic action and no pledges.

The Liberals did not hope to win the election on their
legislative programme. So far as they had one it was to
extend the franchise, redistribute seats on a basis closer to
'one vote, one value', and relax the laws of settlement and
entail. The programme was set out in an article in the *Edinburgh Review*, called 'Plain Whig Principles', though it was
not officially acknowledged. Hartington received Reeve the
editor at Chatsworth and told him what ought to be said, but
seems not to have been pleased by the result; when Reeve
wrote and asked if the article was satisfactory, Hartington
was a little puzzled to know what to say, and hoped nobody
knew that he had inspired it. Whatever it was like as an
article, as a programme it was very sensible. The few Liberals
such as Lowe and Goschen, who opposed extending the
franchise were remarkable for eminence rather than numbers and the Radicals could feel it was a step in the right
direction even if it did not go very far.[1]

This does not mean it was in the least exciting. Redistribution was altogether too complicated and too painful to
be referred to in public and in 1884 it eventually had to be
handed to a committee. Extension of the franchise was discussed more than in 1865, 1910, and 1924, but the mere
mention of these dates is enough to show how little attention
has been paid to extension of the franchise in electing the
successive Parliaments that have carried it out. Treating the
county householder on the same basis as the borough householder was a simple idea, and one that very few people cared
to oppose, but it did not arouse enthusiasm and may have
awakened a few doubts in county constituencies in which
farm-labourers were not highly thought of.[2]

[1] 'Plain Whig Principles', *Edinburgh Review*, Jan. 1880; Hartington to Granville, 19 Jan.: P.R.O. 30–29–27.

[2] Speeches of Forster, Bright, and Hartington, *The Times*, 22 and 24 Mar.,
2 Apr.; even so the *Pall Mall Gazette* was probably justified in saying there was
'no question to which reference had been more rare' than the county franchise,
7 Apr.

Government finance was discussed at much greater length. People believed that a government could overspend its income and go bankrupt, just like a private person. If anyone doubted this, he had only to look at the fact that Turkey had defaulted, and had helped to bring on the Eastern crisis by doing so; by 1880 Egypt was going the same way. The Liberals had always accepted the need for financial rectitude when they were in office; Gladstone had said a government should show a surplus in good times and break even in bad times, and nobody disagreed. It could be argued by a modern economist that Northcote's approach was more up to date: he was unwilling to increase the burden of taxation in bad times, he expanded the floating debt by issuing Exchequer Bills as a form of short-term loan, and he made loans to municipal enterprises which he then reckoned as part of the Treasury's assets. All this may have been very sensible, but Northcote was certainly not the man to explain a new system of finance even if he had thought there was any novelty about it, and most of the electorate saw his policy as a compromise with moral evil in the form of debt. Speakers and pamphleteers hurried into the field, proclaiming the dubious major premise that figures cannot lie and are an excellent way to test the worth of a government, and going on to produce figures which proved that this was the worst, or alternatively the best, of governments.[1]

The figures for the National Debt were an obvious place to start. The Liberals had paid off £20 million in five years of office; the Conservatives tried to show that they had also done so, but could manage this only by including the steady payment of terminable annuities which were an unavoidable charge and were not normally brought into this sort of calculation. Northcote had set up a Sinking Fund, to reduce the Debt by £650,000 a year at first, and subsequently by the amount of interest due on the redeemed stock as well. The depression, with its consequent fall in revenue, defeated the plan, for no surplus was available. The Conservative deficit, with its accumulation of floating debt, was the theme of many Liberal speeches, and they showed no readiness to

[1] Speeches of Gladstone, *The Times*, 29 Apr. 1879; speech of Northcote, ibid., 26 Mar. 1880.

accept the Suez Canal shares or the municipal loans as assets to be set against the debts.[1]

The Liberals estimated the total deficit under the Conservatives at £8 million, and compared it unfavourably with the surplus gained between 1868 and 1874; the Conservatives replied that this showed the Liberals had been altogether too willing to impose taxation. They supported this by showing that for the period of Liberal government the total level of income-tax had been 1s. 10d., while for an equal period of Conservative government it had been only 1s. 8d. There may have been enthusiasts who remembered this, but most people were more likely to remember that taxation had declined under the Liberals and had risen under the Conservatives, and that even so Northcote had not raised taxation to the level needed to wipe out the deficit.[2]

The idea of financial honour exercised quite a number of Liberals, and events after the election show the importance it had for them. Once assured of the premiership Gladstone took the Exchequer as a second post for himself. The City of London had voted Conservative, but it responded to his decision: the slight rise in Consols that followed may have been a coincidence, but at least it showed that he had not brought the ruin and Radical revolution that had been prophesied. In his Budget he tried to help the farmers by providing the long-promised abolition of the Malt Tax, and at the same time to restore 'honesty' to the national accounts by raising the income-tax to sixpence; at the time so much attention was paid to a balanced Budget, and the government's direct effect on the National Income was so slight, that the deflationary implications of this tax increase were probably outweighed by the restoration of business confidence.[3]

The Liberals claimed that they would not only provide honest but also cheaper government. It was hard to compare expenditure from 1868 to 1874 with the 1874 to 1880 period: in the first place Liberal legislation had increased

[1] Speeches of Northcote, *The Times*, 12 Mar., 1 and 6 Apr.; speech of Lowe, ibid., 26 Mar.; speeches of Sandon and of Hartington, ibid., 23 Mar.

[2] Address of Harcourt, ibid., 16 Mar.; the City Liberals, ibid., 26 Mar.; speeches by Hicks-Beach and Lord George Hamilton, ibid., 31 Mar. and 1 Apr.

[3] *The Economist*, 1 May; *Annual Register for 1880*, p. 89.

the burden on the Exchequer of education and local government, and in addition there were some expenses which
involved judgements about government policy. Gladstone
said the *Alabama* damages should be excluded because they
were non-recurring and non-controversial; this reminded
everybody that the Conservatives had joined in the arbitra-
tion that led to the assessment of the claims, and left it open
to the Liberals to place the £6 million vote of credit of 1878
to the account of the government. The claim was that,
although it was a non-recurring expense, it could not be
excluded because the policy on the Eastern Question which
led to the vote of credit had not been accepted by both parties.[1]

Selectiveness of this sort naturally made the balance sheet
particularly unfavourable to the Conservatives. Their active
foreign policy meant they had inevitably incurred larger
costs of this sort, and Gladstone was blaming them for it
twice over, once for having an unsatisfactory foreign policy
and once for spending money on it. But even if all non-
recurring costs had been omitted a basic Liberal case would
have remained: under the Conservatives the costs of administrative duties performed by governments in both periods had
increased. As the figures came out more attractively for the
opposition if the non-recurring costs were not omitted, this
was the form in which the Liberals presented them.[2]

Very probably the increase in administrative costs was the
result of an increase in government activity, but it was suggested that the Conservatives were less practised administra-
tors than the Liberals. They had been out of office for most
of the last thirty years, their Cabinet contained a very large
proportion of peers and country gentlemen sitting for county
seats, and they certainly did not possess the sternness and
energy with which Gladstone and Lowe saved candle-ends:
the implication was that the taxpayers' money was being
wasted.[3]

---

[1] Addresses of Goschen and Childers, *The Times*, 12 and 13 Mar.; speeches of
Smith and Northcote, ibid., 26 Mar. and 1 Apr. Gladstone's preface, *Speeches in
Scotland*, i. 3.

[2] 'Liberal and Conservative Finance' and 'The Government and the State of
Trade'. National Liberal Club pamphlets, vols. 315 and 6110. 'A Political Handbook for the People', B.M. 8139 aaa 5.

[3] Brodrick's pamphlet 'Liberal Principles' said (inaccurately) that all the Cabinet,

The taxpayers were in no mood to see their money being wasted. The depression which lay so heavily on them was obviously the issue behind much of the discussion of finance, and while nobody said that governments were responsible for depressions, it is clear that a lot of people voted against the Conservatives because of the depression. The figures for income-tax, for government expenditure, and for debt that were being discussed were trivial by modern standards, and government financial operations were in fact on too small a scale to affect the economy.

The Liberals did find ways to suggest that the government was the architect of everybody's misfortunes. Finance was of course the dominant domestic topic in Gladstone's mind, and the Edinburgh Corn Exchange speech of 29 November 1879, delivered to an audience of 4,700, may reasonably be considered one of the most important speeches in the two campaigns. In it he permitted himself considerable freedom of denunciation.

> I am bound to say that I do not believe that Her Majesty's government have entirely stopped the growth of wealth in this country, which the industry and enterprise of the country have brought about. . . . Whereas formerly, under all governments, [the yield of a penny on the income-tax] increased at the rate of £34,000 a year, since the present Government came in, it has increased at the rate of £16,000 a year. It is idle for the Chancellor of the Exchequer to say that he has not stopped the growth of wealth in the country. In six years he has disposed of half of it, let them give him another six years at the dissolution, and depend on it he will go far to dispose of the other half.[1]

This was perhaps his most clear-cut statement that the government was responsible for the depression, but in his letter telling the electors of Midlothian that he proposed to contest the seat he had already linked the issues of foreign policy and finance to the greater condemnation of the government.

The management of finance, the scale of expenditure, the constantly-growing arrears of legislation, serious as they are, only lead

except Gathorne Hardy who sat for Cambridge University, were peers or county Members: National Liberal Club pamphlets, vol. 6110. Bright thought county Members unbusinesslike: *The Times*, 25 Mar. W. H. Smith was a borough Member and sat in the Cabinet from 1877.   [1] *Speeches in Scotland*, i. 78–79.

up to still greater questions. I held before, as I have held in the House of Commons, that the faith and honour of the country have been gravely compromised in the foreign policy of the Ministry. That by the disturbance of confidence, and lately even of peace, which they have brought about, they have prolonged and aggravated the public distress.[1]

If this argument was accepted, there was almost no need for Liberals to add that the Cabinet had violated the rules of parliamentary control of expenditure in order to produce their surprises. Probably the Liberals who spoke about this were primarily concerned for the constitution, but their listeners could easily have gathered that Conservative finance, as well as Conservative foreign and constitutional policy deserved criticism.

The government had little to say about the depression. Cross said that the Liberals should have damped down the economy when prosperity was rising by leaps and bounds, but he did not suggest how it should have been done. Other Conservatives raised the contradictory claim that the Liberals had obtained large surpluses by overtaxing, and the best they could do was to say that governments did not cause depressions. This was true, but it was not likely to save the government of the day.[2]

By 1880 the depression had spread to the countryside, and the mildly anti-landlord programme of the Liberals was more likely to attract support than usual. The Conservatives were expected to be the farmers' friends, but in office they had done so little that the Liberals could ask the farmers to trust a reforming government for once. And in the countryside they had reforms to offer; free trade and financial straightforwardness added nothing to the industrial situation, but they were principles which would produce changes if applied to the countryside. At the simplest level Liberals denounced the fallacy of Protectionism and pointed out—without stressing the difference between farmers in a food-exporting and farmers in a food-importing country—that it had done the

[1] Gladstone's letter to Cowan, 30 June 1879. The letter was reproduced in facsimile so that a copy could be sent to every Midlothian voter: Add. MSS. 44765, ff. 142–3.

[2] Speech of Cross, *The Times*, 22 Mar.; speech of Stanley, ibid., 31 Mar.; '6 Years of Conservative Government', *National Union Pamphlet*, no. 43.

American farmers no good. Liberal economic principles were more relevant to the situation when they were used to justify action on behalf of the tenant farmer. The Game Laws forbade him to shoot the game on the land he rented, and his crops naturally suffered. This was a ready-made subject for Liberal attacks on the monstrous privileges of landlords, and it could be combined with a perfectly realistic offer to help the tenant farmer. The Liberals' order of social values made them willing to restrict the landlords' rights, and the pressure of agricultural depression made it seem high time to sacrifice sport to the farmers' need to produce as much as possible.[1]

In the past poor crops had meant high prices, but so much American corn was coming from the Middle West that prices did not rise, and the farmers could survive only by maintaining a high and steady level of production. If tenants had enjoyed the freedom of industrialists to borrow from the bank they might have been able to increase their efficiency, but the custom had always been for the landlord to finance most improvements, which was why he was not required to compensate departing tenants for any improvement they had made. In Ulster the tenant had some right in the improvements he carried out, and the Conservatives' Agricultural Holdings Act had declared that in England the presumption was that the tenant should be compensated. The Liberals said the Act should be made more stringent so that landlords could not avoid its consequences in the way they had done.[2]

The land laws made it impossible for banks to finance farmers, because the Law of Distress gave the landlord a prior claim on the farmer's assets in case of bankruptcy. They also made it difficult for banks to finance landlords, because settlement and entail tied up many estates so tightly that they could not be alienated to pay debts. The estates were usually settled so that they descended intact to the eldest son, and as

[1] Gladstone's speech of 27 Nov., *Speeches in Scotland*, i. 50–51; speeches of Bright, Hartington, and Harcourt, *The Times*, 24, 25, and 26 Mar. 'Farmers' Grievances', National Liberal Club pamphlets, vol. 6110, estimated that £20 million a year was lost because of the Game Laws.

[2] Speeches of Gladstone, Hartington, and the tenant farmer Howard, *The Times*, 19, 25, and 29 Mar. Giffard gave some support to this view but Cross and most Conservatives opposed it, ibid., 23 and 26 Mar.

a result many landlords felt they should spend their income providing for the other children rather than improving the estate and increasing its value for the heir. Some Liberals may have wanted to change the land laws in order to hurt the landlords, but their programme was, at least on the face of it, merely designed to help the tenant finance improvements.[1]

The Conservatives said the Liberals were trying to set landlords and tenants at variance, and this was probably easier to manage in 1880 than it had been earlier. If landlords and tenants were to disagree the Liberals would gain; Beaconsfield produced a theory of three incomes from land, to show that the landlord was a necessary source of finance, but this was so ill received that it was mentioned in the campaign only by Liberals who wanted to attack it. They had the great advantage that they did not care very much if they offended the small landlords, however much they had to respect the social position of the Whig nobility, and so they could promise much more for the tenants. The Conservatives said they would abolish the Malt Tax, but they had said that in 1874 and had done nothing about it. They also talked about the reform of local government, which for them meant reducing local taxation; Liberals who discussed the issue usually wanted elective County Boards.[2]

The farming community did not suddenly transfer its allegiance to the Liberals in great numbers, for that is not the way opinion moves. Liberals came forward in constituencies thought unpromising in 1874; tenant farmer candidates came forward with no official attachment to either party, though their proposals led them towards the Liberals. They had more detailed ideas than most of the Liberals, and were less ready to propose changes that would directly undermine the position of the land-owners. Thomas Duckham, the most prominent of these candidates, was elected for Herefordshire on a programme of reducing local taxation,

[1] 'What Land Reformers Want', National Liberal Club pamphlets, vol. 6246; 'The Agricultural Depression', *Edinburgh Review*, Jan. 1880; *Spectator*, 21 and 28 Feb. Bradlaugh's Land Nationalization meeting, *Daily News*, 11 Feb.

[2] Beaconsfield's speech, Monypenny and Buckle, op. cit. vi. 498-9; addresses of Brand, Hicks-Beach, and W. W. B. Beach, *The Times*, 13 and 19 Mar.; speech of Lord John Manners, ibid., 24 Mar.

altering the Law of Distress, providing compensation for improvements and adjusting the Corn Averages for calculating tithes. While he seems to have shared a number of Roebuck's views—which meant he disliked Russians, the Church of England, and government waste—he stuck to agricultural questions in his speeches.[1]

For a representative of agricultural interests, in a constituency suffering severely from agricultural depression, this seems a very reasonable attitude; people who disagreed about the Eastern Question might reach agreement on questions of more immediate interest to them. But it is clear from speeches and letters to the newspapers that people thought he ought to have views on foreign policy.[2] This may well have been the feeling of a minority, but it was the minority that felt most interest in politics. Duckham's comparative failure to avoid the issue of foreign policy is only a particularly striking example of the way that, in some people's minds, it was the only question of any importance.[3] This minority contained the people who worked in party organizations and brought the less vocal majority to vote. The majority did not express its views, and was probably influenced by the depression,[4] but there is every reason to believe that foreign policy was the question to arouse those who felt deeply about national honour or the dictates of morality.

[1] The Herefordshire election can be followed in the *Hereford Times*, the *Hereford Journal*, and the *Hereford Mercury*.

[2] *Hereford Journal*, 14 Feb. and 27 Mar.; *Hereford Times* and *Hereford Mercury*, 20 and 27 Mar.

[3] See the disagreement between Lord Rendlesham and the editor of the local paper about whether foreign policy was the most important issue in the election: *East Suffolk Gazette*, 13 Mar.

[4] A letter in the *Pall Mall Gazette*, 7 Apr., sums up a good deal of correspondence from the avowedly non-political.

III

PARTY ORGANIZATION

UNTIL the eighteen-seventies 'the choice of candidates and management of electoral affairs had been in the hands of quite independent and self-nominated local committees, who corresponded when necessary with the party Whips, but formed no part of any larger association or federation'.[1] Probably most constituencies were organized by this sort of committee in 1880, but the National Union of Conservative Associations and the National Liberal Federation had appeared on the scene and were beginning to transform it. In themselves the Union and the Federation might not have been very important and they might have settled down to providing a more efficient version of the co-ordination carried on from the Whip's Offices, but the sort of local organizations they brought together were different from the traditional committees. The old committees had to find a candidate, the new ones had to select a candidate: in the parts of the country where self-nominated committees were the rule, suitable candidates were scarce, but in the regions where the new sort of committee flourished, candidates were relatively plentiful. Self-nominated committees were to be found in the countryside or in towns not much affected by the 1867 extension of the franchise; the Second Reform Bill made new organizations necessary for some constituencies, though it was not inevitable that the new local organizations should federate on a national basis.

The National Liberal Federation, launched by Joseph Chamberlain with the help of Gladstone at a Birmingham mass meeting on 31 May 1877, was the new development of the election so far as organization went, but to some extent it was a response to the National Union which had taken the field at the previous election. Conservative Working Men's Clubs, such as the London and Westminster Working Men's Association organized by W. H. Smith, had been set up

[1] B. Holland, *Life of the Eighth Duke of Devonshire* (London, 1911), i. 244.

very soon after the 1867 Act. Westminster was won by the new organization, though its subsequent transformation from a Radical stronghold probably owed a great deal to population shifts. The London and Westminster Working Men's Association went on to help other similar organizations in setting up the National Union.[1]

At the time the National Union was forming itself to help the Conservative party, Liberal opponents of the 1870 Education Act were forming the National Education League as a pressure group in favour of non-denominational education. Organizing the League gave Chamberlain some standing among advanced Liberals, and he went on to produce a Radical programme much more violent and much more detailed than anything suggested in the next ten years. He described Gladstone's election address in 1874, which made the income-tax the central issue of the campaign, as the 'meanest public document' published on such an occasion.[2] His position was helped by the electoral prestige gained by 'Birmingham methods', which brought success in marshalling the voters and success in raising the morale of the organization. In the first School Board elections held in 1870 on the cumulative vote system, the Birmingham non-denominationalists put up fifteen candidates for fifteen seats, but their denominationalist opponents concentrated their strength and elected nine candidates. In 1873 the non-denominationalists also concentrated their strength, and elected their list of eight.[3] After this the Birmingham Liberals were ready to handle a new situation in parliamentary elections. Although there were three seats to fill, each man had only two votes to cast, but as the Liberals had more than three-fifths of the electorate behind them, it was mathematically possible for them to win all the seats; the novelty was the Ballot Act, which prevented the organizers telling the voters which Liberal was running badly. But in

[1] 'Conservative Reorganisation', *Blackwood's Magazine*, June 1880; R. T. McKenzie, *British Political Parties* (London, 1955), pp. 150–1; Minutes of the 1874 Conference of the National Union.

[2] In 'The Next Page of the Liberal Programme', *Fortnightly Magazine*, Oct. 1874.

[3] J. L. Garvin, *Life of Chamberlain* (London, 1932), i. 123–6 and 256; F. H. Herrick, 'The Origins of the National Liberal Federation', *Journal of Modern History*, xvii (1945).

1874 the Conservatives put forward no candidates, because they expected the Liberals could instruct their supporters who to vote for. The Liberal organization had not understood the new situation in 1870 but by 1874 the central machinery was thought to be strong enough to get voters to 'Vote as you're told'.[1]

This success of organization, which gave Birmingham a good deal of prestige among Liberals, was accompanied by success in making the party workers feel they had some influence inside the party. The three innovations in voting procedure introduced between 1867 and 1872—of which the Ballot has alone survived[2]—with which Birmingham had to deal were not in themselves great hindrances to organization: what they did was to give the Birmingham men a spectacular chance to show their efficiency and the enthusiasm that underlay it. This enthusiasm was due in large measure to the way anybody could aspire to play some part in the direction of the political life of his town under the Birmingham system and could rise to a position where he might have some voice in choosing the candidate and even in recalling him to the party line after he had been elected. Representatives of the wards were elected to a central organization called the Six Hundred at Birmingham, the Two Hundred or Nine Hundred and so on at other places. The Hundreds decided policy, and elected a Management Committee to handle day-to-day affairs.[3]

Gladstone and Granville discussed the new organization in May 1877, when Granville asked Gladstone not to speak at the inauguration of the National Liberal Federation. Gladstone replied that he just wanted to improve the organization. Granville hoped that this would not look like an encouragement of schism, and Gladstone replied that he was not going to be linked with any Birmingham reformulation of policy but, he believed, improvement of the organization

---

[1] Speech of Bright, *The Times*, 20 Mar. 1880.

[2] The 'minority vote' in three-member constituencies ended with the 1885 redistribution, and the cumulative vote ended with the Schools Boards in 1902.

[3] Thus, the Preston 400, *Daily News*, 10 Mar.; the Sunderland 400, *Morning Post*, 12 Mar.; Chester 200, *Daily News*, 16 Mar. For the Birmingham organization, Garvin, op. cit., pp. 254 and 258, including Chamberlain's comment that 'three-quarters of the great committee of the 600 are working-men'.

would help party unity. Granville admitted the need to improve the central organization, but he clearly remained suspicious. He warned Gladstone that an ex-Prime Minister could not escape the responsibilities of his position, and made it clear that these responsibilities included not being used as the catspaw of a Radical revolt. Gladstone stuck to the question of organization, and said 'applying election principles to local organization is a great stroke in the interests of the party'. However, neither of them seems to have realized the importance of Chamberlain.[1]

Six months later Hartington wrote to Granville: 'I do not feel at all certain that we ought to give in our adhesion to this federation scheme.' And he went on to explain that he was afraid the Birmingham plan would cause the control and direction of the party to fall into the hands of the advanced men, which would mean too much had been sacrificed to improving the organization. He referred to the new organization as 'the Caucus', a nickname applied by people who wished to insinuate that Birmingham methods included all the vices of American political machines.[2] Bryce attacked the charge in 1882 and, even making allowances for his Radical sympathies, his argument appears sound. He attributed corruption in American politics to a system of administration which gave the government a great deal of patronage, and absence of political principle to the absence of any deep dividing issues. He did not refer to the charges that the Birmingham City Council placed its contracts only with Liberals, but on the other hand he did not stress the fervour with which the Federation held its principles: by American standards (or the standards of pre-Chamberlain Birmingham) its corruption was very mild and its devotion to principle intense.[3]

Chamberlain accepted the nickname of 'the Caucus' (and the implied accusation that the N.L.F. was growing powerful) willingly—nobody thought of attacking the National Union for having too much power. The Union went no

---

[1] Granville to Gladstone 5, 16, 18, 21, and 27 May: Add. MSS. 44171, ff. 65–80; Gladstone to Granville 17 and 19 May, and 1 June: P.R.O. 30-29-29.

[2] Holland, op. cit. i. 245.

[3] 'The Caucus in the U.S.A. and in Birmingham', *Fortnightly Magazine*, Nov. 1882.

further into the fields of controversy than to pass a motion of loyal support for Beaconsfield. The experience of the National Liberal Federation suggests that working men were interested in policy, but those who joined the National Union did not try to turn it into a lower-class pressure-group within the party. Of the 472 Associations listed in 1875 a 'considerable number were composed almost entirely of the artisan class', so it was succeeding in rallying Conservative working men. Beaconsfield had become aware of the dangers of condescension across an unbridged class-barrier and said there should be no such name as Working Men's Club. This was quoted with approval at the 1878 conference, and in 1879 one delegate said Clubs must be 'dissociated from the idea of patronage by persons of a higher class'.

Comments after the election suggest the Clubs might have been more enthusiastic if they had discussed policy. Some of them were benefit societies whose members expected to get something tangible for their money and this shaded off into the 'politico-benevolent societies which were confined to the electors of one party and supported by the subscriptions of wealthy men of that party'.[1] Such societies still existed, as can be seen from the discussion of the Stroud Benevolent Society at the 1879 Conference. Delegates after the election thought that more lecturers, more speeches, and cheaper Conservative newspapers were the right way to raise enthusiasm. Both the Union and the Federation were intended to provide a central forum for arousing enthusiasm in local organizations, but the National Union was always in the hands of the leadership and was meant to provide an instrument for getting in touch with an otherwise inaccessible part of the electorate, while the Federation was intended, just as Hartington and Granville feared, to influence the policy of the leadership. The logic of Chamberlain's Hundreds was that there should be only one such organization to a constituency to choose the candidate, but Conservative Associations were not normally expected to choose the candidate, so the fact that the National Union had 310 affiliated Associations against the Federation's 101 does not mean the Union's work was more widespread. The Federation had

---

[1] N. Gash, *Politics in the Age of Peel* (London, 1953), p. 128.

branches—not all calling themselves Hundreds—in 77
constituencies or so, mainly in the West Midlands, Lancashire, Yorkshire, and Durham; 62 of the Associations represented at the 1879 Conference were important enough to
assume the name of their constituency, and 32 of them lay in
this region. Nineteen of the Liberal gains in county seats
were within it.[1]

Neither national organization included all the societies
that might have joined. In 1878 there were 950 Conservative Associations in the country, an increase of 450 since
1872, but as only 266 were affiliated to the National Union
in 1878 the increase was not solely due to its existence. The
London Radicals had Hundreds, though Southwark was the
only one affiliated to the Federation at the time of the election and when it failed very badly in the by-election in
February 1880 Gladstone feared it was only a counterfeit
of the Birmingham organization. Finsbury, Greenwich,
and Marylebone had Hundreds, and the Eleusis Club in
Chelsea was a very similar organization, but they were not
affiliated to the Federation. The Surrey Liberals did not
have Hundreds, but were affiliated, so it seems the Federation neither included all the people who applied election
principles to local organization nor insisted that all its
members should practise them.[2]

The new movements were successful: in 1874 the Union
had Associations in 65 out of the 74 seats the Conservatives
gained in England and Wales, and in 1880 Chamberlain
wrote to *The Times* claiming that the Caucus had triumphed
in 60 out of the 67 boroughs in which it had taken a hand,
and that it had also fought in ten county constituencies and
won seats in all of them.[3] But although successful this
does not mean they always brought peace and quiet, as the
case of Northampton will show. The town had a Liberal

[1] Minutes of Conferences of the National Union, 1874–80; Reports of Conferences of the National Liberal Federation, 1877–80.

[2] Gladstone to Granville, 18 Feb.: P.R.O. 30–29–29. The London organizations
were mentioned at the beginning of the campaign in *The Times*, the *Daily News*,
and the *Morning Post*, all of 10 Mar.

[3] Minutes of the 1874 Conference of the National Union; *The Times*, 13 Apr.
1880 (in this letter Chamberlain seemed less pleased with 'caucus' as a nickname);
H. J. Hanham, *Elections and Party Management* (London, 1959), p. 164.

Association and a Radical Two Hundred which was affiliated to the Federation and was devoted to Charles Bradlaugh, the atheist and agitator. In the general election of 1874 and at the by-election later in 1874 after the death of the Liberal Member he stood as a Radical, dividing the vote and leaving a constituency with a clear Liberal majority in the hands of two Conservatives for over five years.

By 1880 the Liberal Association was resigned to leaving one seat to him. Their own candidate, Ayrton, had been a minister, but complaints were heard that he did not visit the constituency often enough, and a local Liberal called Wright began holding meetings. Ayrton wanted the Liberals and Radicals each to choose a candidate, Bradlaugh wanted a test ballot, and all of them expressed the utmost goodwill. But when Ayrton had a fall while riding and had to withdraw, his supporters asked J. S. Balfour to take up the moderate Liberal cause. The Radicals successfully pressed Balfour to stand at Tamworth, and then took the offensive: Labouchere, a former Member for Middlesex and the editor of *Truth*, was brought forward and selected. As he was a supporter of Disestablishment he could not be called a moderate, and this lends support to Wright's complaint that the Radicals had packed the selection meeting. Wright was persuaded to go to London to put his case before the Whips' Office, and there he accepted the advice of the Whip's brother-in-law— Adam was away in his constituency—that he should stand down. He even spoke at the Liberal eve-of-poll meeting and denied the rumour that he had been paid to stand down. Despite this edifying testimony to party unity the Liberals could not vote together: 3,501 voted for Bradlaugh and Labouchere, but 983 voted for one but not the other. Some of them supported Bradlaugh as a local man, some of them preferred Labouchere as at least a nominal Christian.[1]

Disputes of this sort were not caused by the creation of the National Liberal Federation. Until the Ballot Act it was possible to treat the first hour's voting as a primary, at the end of which the Liberal running second would retire; disputes clearly existed before 1874, though in that election they may have been more bitter than usual. The Radical

[1] This paragraph is based on the weekly *Northampton Mercury*.

groups which ran candidates in 1874 were indispensable foundations for the Federation, but once it was established it saw that one of its duties was to prevent Liberals running against one another. Eleven seats had been lost in this way in 1874, but only one (Tower Hamlets) in 1880. Sergeant Simon, the sitting Member for Dewsbury, had a Radical as well as a Conservative opponent, but beat both of them easily. The Conservatives had no such problems: normally their candidates were selected without open disputes, and the selection conference at Tynemouth, which adopted the candidate by 52 votes to 38, was most unusual.[1] The National Union was not a body committed to a particular brand of Conservatism, so its appearance was not a symptom of division.

On the other hand, the Radical Associations were powerful only if they could find candidates. In Finsbury the Three Hundred opposed the renomination of Torrens but could find nobody to stand against him; one of the people they had invited, Lord Ramsay, was also put forward (successfully) in Liverpool by the Nine Hundred, and Rathbone, the Liberal 'minority clause' Member, was compelled to retire. At Bradford, Forster, who had been opposed by two Liberals in 1874 after his Education Act, was left in peace though this may have been the result of representations by the Liberal party leaders. In Scotland disputes were more common: in East Aberdeenshire Gladstone and Hartington acted as arbitrators, Adam persuaded a Liberal candidate in Caithness to stand down, and in St. Andrews a trial ballot of Liberal voters was held. However, these may have been problems natural in a one-party region. In the Radical areas of England some breakdown of social inhibition had taken place which provided a large enough number of candidates for the Hundreds to make a choice.[2]

The pre-1867 constituencies in England had been small enough and sufficiently dominated by the upper ranks of society for influential men to stand out as obvious members

[1] Nuffield Collection, quarto vol., has a ballad about this selection conference.
[2] Finsbury, *The Times*, 10 and 12 Mar.; Liverpool, ibid., 17 Mar., and *Globe*, 17 Mar.; Bradford, Wemyss Reid, *Life of Forster* (London, 1889), pp. 342–8; Scotland, *Pall Mall Gazette*, 27 Jan., and *The Times*, 1 and 17 Mar.

of a committee without any process of election.[1] Only a small number of people possessed the social weight which was indispensable for a candidate in these constituencies,[2] and of course not all of these people wanted to become candidates. In North Northamptonshire, the Hon. Robert Spencer, who was only twenty-two but possessed a position in the county, took a little persuading; in North Derbyshire no second Liberal candidate could be found by the committee and an indignation meeting was held; in West Gloucestershire 3,600 pledges of votes were produced when Lord Moreton asked for proof of support; and in West Kent none of this would work, and the Liberals had to run a lawyer provided by the Whips' Office. The Conservatives had little difficulty in the countryside, but in Sheffield they tried without success to persuade Mr. Firth, a very generous local benefactor, to stand. Mr. Gladstone was, of course, sought after: he told the Liberals of Leeds he could not accept their offer because of the reasons he had given for leaving Greenwich, but he was clearly attracted by Midlothian. Adam guarded his interests, kept Leeds open, obtained canvass returns from Midlothian and warned him not to accept Midlothian too quickly lest faggot votes be created against him.

The experiences of the Liberals of North and East Devon illustrate the difficulties of a party organization in an area in which invitations to stand were still issued. When Mr. Cave, the senior Liberal member for Barnstaple, withdrew after the election had begun, the local Liberals unsuccessfully approached

---

[1] M. Ostrogorski, *Democracy and Political Parties* (London, 1902), i. 151–3, has an idealized account of these committees. *The Times*, 23 Apr., argued that Caucuses were merely more formal section committees.

[2] A few exceptions were appearing even in the most rural counties. When a South Lincolnshire clergyman protested at the effrontery of a garden-seed shopkeeper standing as a Liberal candidate for the constituency, the shopkeeper replied that he hoped to sit in the Commons with the owner of the bookstall on Grantham Station (i.e. W. H. Smith), *Daily News*, 7 Apr. The county families still had a great deal of power; people's attention was caught by the tenant farmer Laycock in North Lincolnshire, who withdrew and then presented himself again at the last minute, but it seems that his success was due to the fact that the Yarborough influence, quiescent in 1874, was active on the Liberal side again. W. Saunders, *The New Parliament of 1880* (London, 1880), p. 240; Hanham, op. cit., p. 27.

[3] *Northampton Mercury*, 7 Feb.; *New Mills and Hayfield Advertiser*, 19 Mar.; *Morning Post*, 25 Feb.; *The Times*, 25 Mar.; *Cambridge Examiner*, 3 Apr.; Adam to Granville, 13 Jan. 1879, in letters from Gladstone: P.R.O. 30-29-29, and Adam to Gladstone, 3, 10, and 17 Jan. 1879: Add. MSS. 44095, ff. 70–73 and 77.

Mr. Batten, Mr. Petter, and Lord Ebrington (in that order). Then they turned to the Whips' Office for a candidate, and were provided with H. R. Grenfell, a member of the committee of the Central Liberal Association. He must have seemed a very fair match for Sir Robert Carden who had been supplied as a 'gentleman from the Carlton'[1] for a by-election two months earlier. Perhaps because the electorate respected his years (he was 79), perhaps because he had invested heavily in their goodwill during the by-election, Carden was successful.[2]

Ebrington might have seemed an ideal partner for Lord Lymington, who had won the February by-election, and it was taken for granted that he could have won a seat in Barnstaple, or North Devon, or probably East Devon, but he had a multitude of good reasons for not standing: he was a moderate Liberal who was said to approve of the government's foreign policy, he did not want to spend money campaigning, and he was a friend of Sir Thomas Acland, the Liberal member for North Devon. Acland wanted Ebrington to stand in reserve, and his calculations show the way social prestige and personal popularity had made Ebrington into an undefeatable candidate and demonstrate how things were settled without reference to a formal party organization. As soon as Ebrington committed himself to any of the three constituencies, another Conservative would stand with Sir Stafford Northcote and Acland would be defeated. But as Ebrington could be elected in North Devon, there was no point in the Conservatives putting up a second candidate as long as he remained only a potential candidate, because he could step forward and nullify their efforts. On the other hand, if the Conservatives held back, he would also hold back, and this would mean Northcote and Acland could divide the seats without the expense of a contest. These expenses were not inconsiderable: when asked to stand for East Devon Ebrington asked the constituency Association to guarantee his expenses up to £4,000. Initially they could offer only £2,500, and before they could find any more, Acland had persuaded Ebrington to retire.[3]

---

[1] For this phrase, see 'Conservative Disorganisation', *Fortnightly Magazine*, Nov. 1882.

[2] *Manchester Guardian*, 11 Mar.; *Exeter and Plymouth Gazette*, 23 and 24 Mar.

[3] Ibid., 13, 16, 17, and 20 Mar., and 8 Apr. See Hanham, op. cit., p. 21.

The average candidate spent about £3,000 in a contested English county, so he was asking for a larger sum than usual, but he may have wanted to put the Association off or he may have feared an expensive contest. The highest expenditure was £12,738. 14s. 8d. incurred by a candidate standing without a partner, the highest by a pair of candidates was £15,531. 15s. 8d. and the total in the costliest struggle was £25,782. 1s. 8d. Noble families were unlikely to be bankrupted by these sums as they had been by contests in the previous century, but only wealthy men could stand unless their expenses were guaranteed. The boroughs, as well as being socially more tolerant, were cheaper to contest, but even so a candidate could not be returned without heavy expenditure unless he was supported by an organization of the new sort which was supported by party zeal. The inexpensive return of Fawcett was a sign that zeal was remarkably cheap, if only it could be aroused. At the time Radicalism seemed to awaken it better than anything else.[1]

As a compliment or an inducement to a favoured candidate, the Association might pay his expenses: the Leeds Liberals had Gladstone elected without his doing anything to encourage them openly which might give the impression he did not take Midlothian seriously, and his Midlothian expenses were also paid. His son Herbert had his expenses paid in Middlesex, but when Northcote's son stood in Exeter he paid his own expenses, and this was more usual. Some candidates paid subscriptions to local charities or made generous gifts to the constituency at large. This need not imply corruption; a gentleman is expected to be openhanded. When the Conservative candidate in North Leicestershire declined to renew his subscription to the Keadby Regatta because he had lost, the Secretary very reasonably replied: 'I am at a loss to imagine what connection there is between your candidature and the Regatta held at this place. The connection in which you place the two implies a motive on your part which is far from honourable.'[2]

---

[1] Figures for expenditure, *Parl. Papers*, 1880, lvii. 1.
[2] Adam to Gladstone, 15 Jan. 1879 and 20 Mar. 1880: Add. MSS. 44095, ff. 75–76 and 105–6; Gladstone's explanation, *The Times*, 20 Mar.; Northcote to Salisbury, 19 Apr. 1880: Christ Church papers; W. Saunders, op. cit., p. 241.

Expenses of this sort have of course no place in the official returns of election expenses but the recorded figures indicate the scale on which the battle was fought. Candidates were required to submit accounts to the Returning Officer, and outside Ireland they almost all did.

	Opposed Conservatives	Unopposed Conservatives	Opposed Liberals	Unopposed Liberals
England:	£	£	£	£
boroughs	334,174	176	308,144	2,198
counties	396,921	11,669	275,699	3,308
Wales:				
boroughs	16,415		15,025	799
counties	45,586	492	21,926	1,045
Scotland:				
boroughs	32,468		20,192	1,554
counties	63,648		56,492	2,360
	£889,215	£12,338	£697,414	£11,268[1]

These figures amount to £1,610,236 and the university expenses and those of the independent candidates only raise the total for Great Britain to £1,620,379. The published accounts suggest that the Conservatives outspent the Liberals especially in the counties. There were complaints after the

[1] *Parl. Papers*, 1880, lvii. 1; ibid., 1883, liv. 369 divides up the electorate:

COUNTY VOTERS

	£12 occupier	£50 tenant	40s. freeholder	Total	Out-voters *
England	330,758 + 3,215	85,425	477,645	897,043	90,681
Wales	25,586	7,509	36,581	69,678[sic]	4,183
Scotland	[54,987]		44,665	99,652	7,528
Ireland	154,778		[11,219]	165,997	4,875
	566,109	92,934	570,110	1,229,153	107,267

BOROUGH VOTERS

	Householders	Lodgers	Others (freemen, etc.)	Total
England	1,524,169	21,664	36,533	1,582,366
Wales	68,056	254	1,056	69,366
Scotland	184,813	323	25,653	210,789
Ireland	51,003	1,213	5,805	58,021
	1,828,041	23,454	68,657	1,920,542

The county franchise in Scotland and in Ireland was not strictly comparable with that in England and Wales.

election that prosperous Conservative counties had declined to help needy boroughs nearby. On the whole Conservative supporters were probably richer than Liberals, though the wealthiest individual landlords, the rich men with money not tied up in land, and the nonconformists accustomed to giving to charities and public causes, were on the Liberal side.

The accounts returned are not all-inclusive. Expenditure in Ireland was probably not very important, but money spent without being reported to the Returning Officer may have been considerable. Commissions investigating corrupt practices suggest that in corrupt boroughs only a half or a third of the expenses might be returned; in less corrupt boroughs, which were usually larger, expenses were probably understated without too much intent to break the law; and in counties landlords might do favours, such as carrying out repairs, which could not be recorded. Petitions in counties were infrequent, so it is hard to find what returnable expenses were omitted. Estimates that three-quarters or four-fifths of the total expenses were recorded seem reasonable enough, and this would mean a total expenditure of something over two million pounds. In 1883 one Member suggested a figure of three million pounds, but he did not make it clear whether this implied a high level of unreturned expenses or was an attempt to include pre-election payments. However, his estimate of about £1 spent per voter in the election cannot be very far off the mark,[1] though it may be a little on the high side.

These figures for total expenditure illustrate the unimportance of the official central machinery. Mr. Hanham has shown that the Liberal Whips' Office had about £33,000 to spend; Lord Cork raised an additional Liberal fund, which Hanham does not mention, of about £6,000; and the newspaper estimates of the Conservative equivalent, the Carlton

---

[1] Only 93 out of 172 candidates in Ireland submitted their expenses. Speech of de Ferrieres, 3 *Hansard* cclxxix. 1672. The whole debate, cols. 1651–1706, is informative. Note the Attorney General's estimate, col. 1697, that this was the most expensive election ever fought. See also W. B. Gwynn, *Democracy and the Cost of Politics* (London, 1962), p. 51. George Howard to Granville, 11 Apr., said Musgrave won East Cumberland because people thought that if he lost they would never have a contest again: P.R.O. 30–29–27.

Fund, run at about £24,000. The Carlton Fund was usually richer than the Whips' Office, so this may be an underestimate, or it may show the Conservatives had not been preparing for the election as carefully as the Liberals. But it seems unlikely that as much as 4 per cent. of the total returned election expenditure can have been provided by the central organizations. The Liberal Whips gave lump sums amounting to something over £2,000 to the Scottish and Irish organization, and quantities ranging from £200 to £1,000 (apart from one loan of £3,000) to thirty-four constituencies. No doubt it was useful, and the constituencies were chosen skilfully, and these payments do not fully account for the central expenditure, but it could not be regarded as important.[1]

Suggestions of very large expenditure by individual Liberals lead into the field of rumour. Lord Rosebery said some time later that he had spent £50,000 on the election; this statement has been subjected to fairly convincing criticism which suggests he had been including the cost of property which he bought to acquire electoral influence in Midlothian. However, it is conceivable that he financed campaigns in several Scottish constituencies and that this was part of the foundation of his political prestige in Scotland. Samuel Morley was said to have provided £20,000, though the only gift from him that can be traced is £500 to Herbert Gladstone. A Liberal Fund organized by the Reform Club was estimated at £200,000 or even £260,000, but even if such a fund existed the figures are certainly too high. There would have been difficulties about paying the money out and the whole structure of power in the party would have been different if it had been financed by a few Whig aristocrats.[2]

Finance was not the business of the central agencies. The Liberal Central Association tried to keep in touch with voters

[1] H. J. Hanham, 'British Party Finance, 1868–80', *Bulletin of the Institute of Historical Research*, 1954; R. B. Brett (Lord Esher), *Journals* (London, 1934), i. 65; Cork to Granville, 1 Apr. seemed to think the figure satisfactory, and Cardwell mentioned that he had given £500 to it, Cardwell to Granville, 23 Mar.: P.R.O. 30–29–27. *World*, 14 Apr.

[2] Diary of Sir Edward Hamilton, 30 June 1882: Add. MSS. 48623. R. R. James, *Rosebery* (London, 1963), pp. 101–2; on Morley, *Whitehall Review*, 24 Apr., and *Globe*, 18 Mar.; *World*, 14 Apr., and *Vanity Fair*, 10 Apr.; J. Vincent, *The Formation of the Liberal Party* (London, 1966), p. 9.

who moved, the Devonshire Club and the Carlton Club kept lists of candidates who could be sent out when local Associations asked for one.[1] The National Union and the National Liberal Federation had no money to spend; they were committees for bringing together constituency organizations which were probably more firmly established than the co-ordinating body. Their balance-sheets are simple enough;[2]

[1] Granville kept a circular from the Association: P.R.O. 30–29–25. The Carlton Club provided money for the Oxford by-election as well as handling the finance for the general election: *Parl. Papers*, 1881, xliv, Report of Royal Commission on the Oxford election.

[2] Minutes of 1880 and 1881 Conferences of the National Union; Annual Reports of the National Liberal Federation, 1879–81.

INCOME

	National Union 1879			1880			National Liberal Federation June 1878– June 1879			June 1880– 1881		
	£	s.	d.	£	s.	d.	£	s.	d.	£	s.	d.
Brought forward	49	8	10	107	8	5	246	4	4	10	15	11
Subscriptions	859	0	6	1,456	14	0	854	19	0	1,431	19	6
Bank Interest	31	0	10	15	10	5	12	11	4			
Sale of Consols				1,042	10	11						
Sale of pamphlets										172	0	1
	£939	10	2	£2,622	3	9	£1,113	14	8	£1,614	15	6

EXPENDITURE

	National Union 1879			1880			National Liberal Federation June 1878– June 1879			June 1880– 1881		
	£	s.	d.	£	s.	d.	£	s.	d.	£	s.	d.
Salaries	100	0	0	75	0	0	452	5	6	548	12	4
Lecturers	103	15	5	133	6	10						
Messenger	18	14	3	12	10	11						
Auditor	2	2	0									
Travelling							171	18	11	81	6	6
Printing, Advertising	290	11	4	1,607	10	11	196	8	1	383	5	0
Conference expenses	137	9	0	7	16	0				289	8	11
Rent	75	0	0	56	5	0	46	8	10	107	7	8
Office	27	6	9	32	19	3				73	17	8
Postage	56	3	0	65	12	5	185	5	10	63	0	0
Pamphlets	21	0	0	21	0	0						
Paid to Secretary				50	0	0				36	12	8
				[testimonial]						[debt from 1880]		
Sundries				4	10	6						
	£832	1	9	£2,066	11	10	£1,052	4	2	£1,583	10	9
Brought forward	£107	8	5	£555	11	11	£61	10	6	£41	4	9

the Liberals did not keep theirs for 1879–80 but it was discussed at their 1881 Conference and was presumably not surprising.

The organizations may have acted as secret channels down which money flowed from well-concealed party funds, but it seems unlikely: the Reform Club would hardly have placed their funds at Chamberlain's disposal, and the Carlton Club was not at ease with the National Union.[1] At most the new organizations might have provided mailing-lists for whatever central funds there were. The Federations were not designed as agencies which could direct operations during an election, and they had no control of party policy. They came to life once a year for conferences which gave party enthusiasts a chance to meet and sustain one another's faith. Holland was probably right in saying the federating organizations, as opposed to the federated, were useful only for giving an appearance of party unity, for organizing big meetings, and for distributing literature, though he might have added that they acted as publishers for this literature and sometimes commissioned pamphlets on their own account. At the Conservative Conference in 1874 the leaders said the object of the Union was to help in the formation and work of the Associations, without trenching on their proper independence. The Federation could have described its position in similar language.[2]

The Federation and the Union had the beginnings of full-time staffs and the tendency towards employing full-time agents for organization instead of solicitors specializing in work on the register was noticeable among the constituent Associations. General Burnaby attributed his election in North Leicestershire to a system of full-time work, a well-organized register and a paid principal agent. This cost £300 a year, which was met by annual subscriptions of 12s. each. A full-time agent paid a salary by the member would be in a difficult position and, if the Association failed to find a candidate, it would also be without a full-time organizer. So it was the Association which pro-

---

[1] Ostrogorski, op. cit. i. 508–9; H. Gorst, *The Fourth Party* (London, 1906), p. 266.

[2] Holland, op. cit. i. 249; Minutes of the 1874 Conference of the National Union.

vided the professional organizers to deal with the increased electorate, and this meant it had machinery in its hands which could be turned against the Member, which led to the weakening of his position deplored by Ostrogorski. The organization could set out to control the member by reminding him that the party had given pledges, and in this way the views of the organization would dictate the Member's actions unless he could arouse supporters of his own.[1]

However, the rapid conversions, under constituency pressure, of the Home Rule period were not likely until the central organization had some control over the Associations. In 1880 the central organizations did not aspire to control the constituencies; they were happy if they could keep in touch with them. Party enthusiasm was dying at the Reform, and the Carlton was not well organized: it served as a reservoir of candidates, but the work of fitting them into constituencies was undertaken by the Central Office. In the years before the 1874 election the office was run efficiently by Disraeli and John Gorst, a young barrister he picked out for the job. After victory Disraeli was too busy as Prime Minister, Gorst felt neglected and resigned, and the office was taken over by Skene, who was not a Member of Parliament and appears to have lacked the social standing necessary for the job.[2]

After the election a great many complaints were heard about Conservative party machinery. Contact between party headquarters and the constituencies was said to be weak, and few good local agents had been found. One critic suggested that area committees should be set up to combat the local jealousies which led people to lose a seat rather than ask for outside help. The writer felt that the laws of libel and good taste prevented his giving examples to show where borough Conservatives had been left in the lurch, but as he also complained that the local leaders of Conservative sentiment, the great families of the neighbourhood, the rank-and-file M.P.s and the influential local gentlemen had

---

[1] Minutes of the 1880 Conference of the National Union; Ostrogorski, op. cit. i. 497–501.
[2] Gorst, op. cit., pp. 3 and 32–36; 'Conservative Reorganisation', *Blackwood's Magazine*, June 1880; 'The Revolutionary Party', *Quarterly Review*, Apr. 1881.

failed in their duty to back the candidate up and educate the voter, he was obviously a hard man to satisfy. His recommendation that a system of constituency agents and district agents should be set up was a recognition that full-time political workers were becoming more important, though it was hardly possible to do anything while money was short. In particular, the boroughs were poor and, though they were necessary for a Conservative victory, the candidates in them were too often men who had just come down from London or rich men who could pay the expenses.[1]

This writer did not discuss the National Union, and another critic said, 'While we admit, from a mere electioneering agent's point of view, the success of the Caucus at the recent election, we would never counsel the adoption of that system by the Conservative Party', because it helped corruption in America and people would not take sufficient interest in electing the 'Hundreds'.[2] But the next stage in the argument over 'Conservative Disorganization' was so closely linked with Lord Randolph Churchill's struggle to control the National Union that it may not be possible to take statements completely at face value. Gorst had declared, at the Conference which discussed the defeat, that it was 'not fair to say their defeat was due to faulty organization . . . [but] . . . compared with the organization of their opponents they were left far behind'; he went on, with Sir Henry Drummond Wolff, a fellow member of the Fourth Party, to publish an anonymous, and understandably ill received, article in the *Fortnightly Review*.[3]

They said too many upper-class members of the party were not concerned about canvassing or the state of the register; in opposition they cared only for demonstrations and speeches, and in office they sacrificed everything to the interests of the landlords and aristocracy. The Conservative boroughs of Lancashire managed without aristocratic help, and they had survived the flood of 1868 and given an example which led to success in 1874. But Conservative

---

[1] 'A Tory View of the Election', *Nineteenth Century*, June 1880.

[2] 'Conservative Reorganisation', *Blackwood's Magazine*, June 1880.

[3] Minutes of the 1880 Conference of the National Union; 'Conservative Disorganisation', *Fortnightly Review*, Nov. 1882.

legislation had not paid enough attention to the social needs of the boroughs and this was why they had voted Liberal in 1880. The party leaders showed no signs of having learnt their lesson, and still seemed concerned for the private interests of their class. The reaction to this attack was so fierce that Lord Randolph was obliged, although it fitted his views of Tory Democracy very well, to repudiate the article by suggesting that, although it was signed Two Conservatives, its authors must have been a pair of dissatisfied Whigs. But the fact that it provoked an infuriated response does not prove that it was not true.[1]

No such instructive articles were written about the Liberal organization: its success was an ample justification of its work. Adam, a Liberal Whip for part of the 1868 government, took on the post of Chief Whip at a time of great difficulty. Arthur Peel had resigned the post after the defeat of 1874, in despair at the divisions in the party. Adam's main task was to hold the parliamentary party together, but he realized that the rapid conversion of the Whips' Office into a central agency at election time was not enough,[2] and he set about finding candidates well in advance. Using the Devonshire Club as his recruiting centre, he had filled up the borough vacancies by the end of 1879, though he told Gladstone he did not want an election just then because the counties were waking up and he was finding candidates for them. In the absence of selection conferences the Whips had a good deal of influence in finding candidates, but they did not have the money or the secretarial assistance to do much more. In an age without typewriters or telephones, in which the duplicated lithograph and the telegram were the only labour-saving devices known to the party organization, the Central Offices spent most of their time writing things out by hand, and probably had difficulty in finding secretarial staff to do this.[3]

If the party machinery was ill suited for combat outside Westminster, so was the party leadership. Accustomed to

[1] Minutes of the 1882 Conference of the National Union.
[2] A. F. Thompson, 'Gladstone's Whips and the General Election of 1868', *English Historical Review*, 1948, shows the old system at work.
[3] See *Daily News*, 13 Apr.; a stencilled Whip for 2 May 1877 and Adam to Gladstone, 12 Dec. 1879: Add. MSS. 44095, ff. 32 and 95–96.

the search for the support of splinter groups inside the House
of Commons up to 1867, the party leaders were not used to
thinking in extra-parliamentary terms, although opinion in
the constituencies was growing more important, or to
directing policy for a general election. The parliamentary
monopoly of power made the Cabinet the only group which
could form a policy for an election, and this was understood
to be part of its duty.[1] Beaconsfield in 1878 demonstrated
that a leader who knew his own mind could do a lot to get his
own way without much support in Cabinet. Lord Granville,
who held a somewhat ill-defined position as leader of the
Liberal party, consulted the members of Gladstone's Cabinet on policy during the 1874–80 Parliament, but he had
less authority in his party than Beaconsfield in his and did
not issue a manifesto for the general election.[2]

Meetings of the parliamentary party were held by both
sides; Beaconsfield found them helpful and pleasant, but
Gladstone adhered to a Peelite notion that ministers should
present a policy to Parliament without canvassing their
Members in advance.[3] When he retired the leaders of the
party clearly did not want the question of the succession to
be settled by a vote of the parliamentary party: his party
leadership was bequeathed to Granville, as leader in the
Lords, and the ex-Cabinet was obviously relieved that
Hartington became leader in the Commons without any
formal contest. Contact with the party outside Parliament
was much harder to achieve: Beaconsfield and Salisbury
were very glad to receive deputations sent by the Conservative Associations, and they both said how much this had
strengthened their diplomatic position. They went on to
stress the need for an efficient party organization, but this
meeting did not set a precedent or provide a way in which
constituency workers could press their views on the government.[4] Conferences to represent all sections of the party were
not held; the Annual Conferences of the National Union

[1] *The Times*, 17 Feb.
[2] Granville to Gladstone, 23 June 1877: Add. MSS. 44171, ff. 84–85. Arthur
Godley, *Reminiscences* (London, 1931), 100.
[3] 'The Conservative Leadership', *Fortnightly Magazine*, Dec. 1882.
[4] *National Union Pamphlet*, no. 36, gives an account of the presentations made
on 6 Aug. 1878.

and the National Liberal Federation represented small and untypical sections of the two parties, and they were not yet seen as reasons for holding more representative meetings. The leaders consulted the interests of their party workers— the Conservative Licensing Act and the Public Worship Regulation Act rewarded two groups which had done a great deal for victory in 1874—but they were a little uneasy about the propriety of going out and addressing the party workers. Gladstone's relative lack of inhibition about it probably strengthened his political position.

One reason for not approaching the party workers was inherent in the nature of contests. For most of the centuries of Parliament's existence unopposed returns have been normal. Sometimes rival candidates came forward; they found it easy enough to decide which of the two parties at Westminster came closest to their views on politics, but their links with their chosen party were loose, and the parties could not send men down from London to attack them. They had no institutions like the 1922 Committee or the meetings of the Parliamentary Labour Party to make it relatively easy for them to affect party policy, and so they did not regard themselves as completely committed to it in the House of Commons.

The corollary to this was that Members did not call themselves Independent in the twentieth-century sense of the term. The only Member of the 1874–80 Parliament to whom reference-books do not attach a party label was the uninfluential Dr. Kenealy. He had appeared as counsel for the Tichbourne Claimant, had been disbarred for the violence of his advocacy, and was returned for Stoke-on-Trent to support the cause. Popular enthusiasm had died out by 1880 and Kenealy came bottom of the poll, as did the only other announced Independent candidate, Malgarini at Chester, who got 16 votes.[1]

Duckham called himself a tenant farmer candidate in Herefordshire, and stuck to farmers' issues and avoided foreign policy. But however independent he may have

[1] For Kenealy, D. Woodruff, *The Tichbourne Claimant* (London, 1957), pp. 401–2 and 415. To some people, the Claimant represented the cause of the masses against the classes, ibid. xv. For Malgarini, Saunders, op. cit., pp. 231–2 and 340.

intended to be, his support came from the Liberals. Of his 2,726 voters, 2,068 gave their other vote to the Liberal candidate, and 545 voted for one or other of the Conservative candidates. The local Tory editor said that Duckham was a Liberal in disguise; the local Liberal editor told his readers to vote for Duckham. The Herefordshire election, and Duckham's success, deserve attention but not because they show the triumph of an Independent candidate or a candidate who did not spend much money. Probably the Conservatives who stood in Truro and in Buckinghamshire as protests against the supineness of the local Associations should also be included in this category: a minority clause Liberal was so likely to be returned in Buckinghamshire that one can understand the absence of official opposition, but the behaviour of the Truro Association, in conceding without a fight a seat that they held, suggests defeatism or disorganization.[1]

Conservatives outside the ministry often promised 'independent support' of Lord Beaconsfield in election addresses, but once elected they voted loyally with their party. One small demonstration of independence occurred shortly before the dissolution: Wheelhouse of Leeds and seven others divided the House on a motion to set up a Select Committee to look into the problems of Protection. Sir Hardinge Giffard hurried out to avoid voting, but apart from that the government was not embarrassed. There was no danger that the opposition would support the motion and turn it into a threat to the government, because no Liberal could vote for anything so Protectionist.[2]

Liberal members had no need to say that they were independent. On lesser things than Free Trade they voted against their party without too much concern. The division on foreign policy in May 1877 still left its scars, though a division on domestic issues, which could have been more serious, did not come into the open. The Conservatives naturally spoke of the 'patriotic Liberals' who supported the government's foreign policy, and treated the large majority

[1] *Hereford Journal*, 20 Mar. and 10 Apr.; *Hereford Times*, 27 Mar.; Address of Charlsey in *The Times*, 23 Mar.; *Globe*, 27 Mar. and 6 Apr.
[2] *Morning Post*, 14 Feb.

in Parliament as a sign that their policies were popular, though the Liberals replied that most of the 'patriotic Liberals' were Irishmen who were denounced as traitors when they spoke of Home Rule.[1]

It was never possible to say what, apart from disapproval of Conservative policy, was the policy of the Liberal Party on the Eastern Question; one cause of this was the difficulty of finding when a party had committed itself to a policy. The absence of party conferences meant that party leaders were denied one useful forum available to their successors, but it was of course normal for party policy to be laid down by their statements and actions: the *Annual Register* said the Liberal Party was committed to making the county franchise the same as the borough because in 1877 Hartington voted for Trevelyan's annual motion on the subject, and it was true that no responsible leader could vote for a policy he did not intend to support with as much of the weight of party discipline as he could bring to bear. Often it was necessary to indicate a future line of policy without being able to find an opportunity to give a vote for it; when Gladstone showed his 'insight into the facts of particular eras, and their relations one to another, which generates in the mind a conviction that the materials exist for forming a public opinion and for directing it to a particular end', he was not always able to express it as definitely as he did in tabling his Resolutions on the Irish Church. His acceptance of the fact that feeling cannot be aroused on a subject simply by making speeches was more reasonable than Bagehot's notion that 'the leading statesmen of a free country have a great momentary power [i.e. a power of giving momentum]. They settle the conversation of mankind. It is they who, by a great speech or two, determine what shall be said or what shall be written for long after. They, in conjunction with their counsellors, settle the programme of their party.' He went on to say that once they have stated what the issues are, the people can decide them but it could not judge a government without some such guidance.[2]

[1] For a list of fourteen Liberal candidates said to support the government's foreign policy, *Globe*, 29 Mar.
[2] *Annual Register for 1877*, pp. 62 and 66; Gladstone's memorandum: Add. MSS.

Gladstone realized that he could not produce support out of nothing in this way, though he did not propose 'the simple acceptance of public opinion'. This view was fairly clearly shared by Salisbury, who told a large meeting at Manchester the year before the election that it was not possible to turn public attention from foreign affairs to the land or the Church. His speech was mainly devoted to a defence of the policy that led to the Treaty of Berlin, but it also contained the statement that the reports of the signing of an Austro-German alliance would be 'glad tidings of great joy'. Beaconsfield had told him about his conversation with Munster, the German ambassador, on the subject of a German alliance, and later added that he believed 'an alliance between the three powers in question at the moment, might probably be hailed with something like enthusiasm'. After the speech Beaconsfield wrote to congratulate him on the conception and the execution, and assured him—quite incorrectly, for nobody showed the least interest in German affairs—that it would have a great effect on public opinion. To make sure none of the benefit was lost, he sent Corry to London to arrange to circulate the speech widely, because he was afraid the Manchester organizers did not understand the importance of getting it distributed.

This would be a good example of leaders deciding policy in conjunction with their colleagues if Salisbury had not made another speech, on the same day, in which he called protective tariffs 'keys to open the door to the access of trade'. This was the argument of the supporters of retaliation followed by reciprocal concessions, so it made possible accusations that the Tories wanted to bring back Protection. Beaconsfield seems not to have commented on this, so Conservatives later accused of Protectionism might well have wished Salisbury had consulted his colleagues before making a speech which, though it did not commit them to a policy, appeared to indicate a possible new departure.[1]

44791, ff. 51. (Gladstone did not claim to have formed opinion on the Eastern crisis: see R. T. Shannon, *Gladstone and the Bulgarian Agitation 1876* (London, 1963), pp. 110–12.) W. Bagehot, *Essays on Parliamentary Reform* (London, 1883), p. 193.

[1] *The Times*, 18 Oct. 1879; Beaconsfield to Salisbury 1 and 19 Oct. 1879: Christ Church papers.

The announcement of the dissolution provided another opportunity for putting forward party policy. Every candidate issued an election address to his constituents, and those of the dozen or so men at the head of the two parties were printed in the news columns of the London newspapers, which meant they reached a national audience. The address of the party leader was studied especially carefully, and some attempt was made to present it as a statement of policy on which the party was united. These addresses pledged the party to try to carry out the policy outlined in them, and the party could claim electoral authority to pass measures included in them such as the Disestablishment of the Irish Church in 1869. The theory of a mandate, under which Members ought not to vote for measures they had not included in the address, was not seriously advanced until 1886.[1]

These questions of policy became more important as time went on. A comparison of the general election of 1865 with that of 1880 shows how difficult it would be to justify Lowe's phrase about 'educating our masters' (if he ever said it). Issues were discussed much less in 1865 than in 1880; Lowe spoke in the 1866 and 1867 debates as if the enfranchisement of householders would lead to an outbreak of corruption and a deterioration in the intellectual level of politics. Instead it led to an outbreak of speechmaking, steadily growing in intensity. Part of this may have been due to the fact that the artisans enfranchised in 1867 were far better educated than Lowe imagined. Part of it was due to Gladstone's work in educating the nation to treat politics more seriously than it had under Palmerston, but there were also two interrelated organizational reasons for the change.

Lord George Hamilton wrote many years later that he had studied elections carefully for nearly fifty years, and he had noticed that the lower the poll the better the Conservatives fared. He conjectured that this was because they were a single party doomed to fail whenever their opponents launched a coalition that would hold together. Gladstone

---

[1] *The Times* printed in its news columns fifteen addresses by leaders between 9 and 17 Mar.; Hartington's committee, ibid., 11 Mar.; the 'mandate', J. Morley, *Life of Gladstone* (London, 1908) i. 675.

warned his audience, at the launching of the National Liberal Federation, that the Conservative Party was easier to keep together than the Liberal, and that the Conservatives would continue to be better organized as long as both parties were led by their richest men.[1]

The fissiparous tendencies of the Liberals were well known before 1867, but until that time they had to be dealt with by drawing together Members inside Parliament. After the Second Reform Bill, principles and policies were the best means of drawing together the units of the Liberal coalition and hurling them as a single body on the outnumbered Conservatives. The Conservative party remained united, but that was not enough. As long as Beaconsfield was in office no backbenchers would trouble the government, and after the defeat the Fourth Party disturbed Northcote but always tried to remain on good terms with the leader in the Lords. The Conservatives still remained a minority party until Home Rule split the Liberals, and had most chance of success when the Liberals failed to find an issue which enabled them to poll their full strength.[2]

Issues provided the Liberal party organization with energy as well as unity. A great deal more work had to be done with the enlarged electorate than had been necessary previously; it had once been possible to run the organization on a basis of men's loyalty to their landlords and employers, supplemented by payment when needed, but the old loyalties and the respectability of money as a political motive-force were declining just at the time the work was increasing. The men who put the arguments in favour of great causes like the ending of atrocities in Bulgaria were not raising issues for party purposes, but it is nevertheless true that the issue gave party workers something to be excited about.[3] Canvassing for a party is not in itself pleasurable, and with changing times the reward for party work grew increasingly intangible. Why it should be that people who are interested in politics

---

[1] Lord George Hamilton, *Reminiscences and Reflections* (London, 1917), p. 65; Report of the First Conference of the National Liberal Federation.

[2] Gorst, op. cit., pp. 100 and 147–50.

[3] 'The first step to a cordial reunion and reconciliation will have been taken when some worthy object is proclaimed', J. Chamberlain, 'The Next Page of the Liberal Programme', *Fortnightly Review*, Oct. 1874.

become excited about foreign policy issues, while ordinary voters regard them as rather unimportant, is still not clear, but it seems to have been the case in 1880 and the tendency goes on to this day. The Conservatives had no shortage of money, but they had no great fund of enthusiasm in 1880; they claimed that in some cases the failure to rally all their supporters was due to over-confidence, but even this suggests that their organization was glad of an excuse not to work.[1]

It is possible that they could have learnt something from the launching of the National Liberal Federation. A meeting of representatives of the clubs and Associations willing to federate was held at Birmingham on 31 May 1877. After the business meeting over twenty thousand people crowded into Bingley Hall to hear Gladstone. He referred to the new organization and gave it his blessing and then, as was natural and normal in any speech he gave at that time, he dealt with the Eastern crisis and denounced the government's policy. He was followed by Chamberlain, who raised the Radical cry of 'Free Church, Free Schools, and Free Land'. However much concentration on details of administration there had been earlier in the day, these statements of political belief aroused enthusiasm and made people feel that the work of organization was devoted to a noble purpose. This spirit of enthusiasm gave the Federation a reason for existence that was lacking in the National Union, where matters of policy were not considered.[2]

The National Federation was something of a cause of strife and friction, and at its Darlington meeting shortly before the election Chamberlain felt it necessary for the value of unity to soften down its Radicalism on domestic issues. Its foreign policy remained unchanged, and presumably did much to convince its members that 'we stand at Armageddon and we battle for the Lord', and provide the energy for the tiresome business of persuading other people to come and vote.[3]

[1] 'The Stump Ministry', *Blackwood's Magazine*, Nov. 1880; 'A Tory View of the Election', *Nineteenth Century*, May and June 1880.

[2] Report of the First Conference of the National Liberal Federation; Garvin, op. cit. i. 260–1; Ostrogorski, op. cit. i. 178; J. Chamberlain, 'A New Political Organisation', B.M. 8138 c c 8(7).

[3] *Daily News*, 4 Feb. 1880.

IV

TAKING THE ISSUES TO THE PEOPLE

POLITICS and the election had, apart from their perennial attractions, something of the appeal as a spectacle that has more recently been shown by organized sport. The county cricket championship had been contested for only a dozen years; the first Test Match was not played until 1882; professional football was recognized in 1885. Newspapers had a great deal of space for politics, and politicians were themselves seen as contestants in a sport. Sometimes fairly literally: the posters in the election supported their candidate by showing him winning in allegorical horse-races, bicycle-races, foot-races and donkey-chasing-carrot-races. The fact that politics was something like a game made party loyalty more important, and party principles less important, than they would otherwise have been, and this made it natural to treat a fine display by a party leader as something like a fine display by a centre-forward. A series of posters called 'The Boxing-Match' showed Beaconsfield and Gladstone laying into each other, but did not link the rounds of the fight to the events of the previous four years. One pamphlet, 'The Grand National Steeplechase', gave advice on horses and jockeys to bet on in the election, favouring Asian Mystery ridden by Mr. Ben to beat The Woodcutter ridden by Mr. Ewart, but the incorrect forecast was a tipster's mistake and not an attempt to win votes for Asian Mystery.[1]

Politics was one of the great public entertainments. The gramophone had hardly appeared, the theatre was not respectable, and although books were respectable there was

---

[1] For an election as a sporting contest, see M. Ostrogorski, *Democracy and Political Parties* (London, 1902), i. 466, and R. C. K. Ensor, *England, 1870–1914*, pp. 1–2. Nuffield College has a useful collection of posters and pamphlets: see posters for Sheffield, Newcastle, Bolton, Dundee, and Cheltenham in the folio volumes; for the pamphlets, see folio vol. i and octavo vol. i. But it is going altogether too far to say that what people wanted in 1880 was 'the election victory itself, as a visceral thrill'. J. R. Vincent, *Pollbooks: How Victorians Voted* (Cambridge, 1967), p. 47.

not a very intense demand for them—in new fiction, the form of publishing that comes closest to entertainment, there were only 607 new titles in 1879. The figures help illustrate the dominance of the great pastime of respectable Victorians, religion; the same publishers' lists contain 775 new volumes of sermons. People were accustomed to long addresses, and a successful speech was likely to have some sermon-like qualities. There were plenty of statesmen with firmly held religious views to satisfy this inclination. Religion was less directly an issue in the campaign than it had been in the two previous elections, when Irish Disestablishment and denominational education had been central issues. The fate of the Balkan Christians was mentioned, though of course the topic was less dominant than during the Bulgarian agitation itself, and there were a few Conservative claims that a Liberal victory would lead to Disestablishment. But while religious issues were not important, politicians could reckon that the electorate (unlike the unenfranchised male population) was religious in inclination. Gladstone presented himself as the leader of a crusade for righteousness rather than a politician looking for expedients, and clearly regarded his opponents as the incarnation of evil. A couple of Liberal pamphlets set out in the form of catechisms can be taken as examples at a less exalted level; they look strained and artificial at the present day, but presumably were entirely familiar to the people of 1880.[1]

Enthusiasm about politics, after the desire for tranquillity shown from 1874 to 1876, had been kept up by mass meetings before the election; it was argued at the time that 'parliament out of Session' was taking over some of the opinion-forming tasks of the House of Commons. A meeting of ten or twenty thousand people was a great political opportunity, and it was admitted to be a great physical strain; Hartington, for instance, apologized to a Manchester meeting because he did not think he could make himself heard. Gladstone's address to 20,000 people in the Waverley Market at Edinburgh during the first Midlothian campaign was the last big meeting before the dissolution. During the

---

[1] *Truth*, 22 Jan.; speech of 25 Nov. 1879, *Speeches in Scotland*, i. 30; National Liberal Club pamphlets, vol. 6239.

election itself meetings would have been unacceptable intrusions on the autonomy of the constituencies.[1]

Candidates began the contest by issuing an address, which was their most important single piece of printed material. An address by a party leader was a party programme as well as a personal appeal, but the ordinary candidate knew that his address was a good opportunity to define the terms on which the battle would be fought in his own constituency. Addresses and, on some occasions, parodies of the opposing address were used as posters. They were usually published in a prominent advertising-space in the local newspaper, on the front page or next to the leading articles in the centre of the paper. If there were two newspapers, candidates would not place much advertising in the columns of the newspaper opposed to them, but they might insert additional advertisements in the paper that supported them: in North Derbyshire the Liberal newspaper carried 'boxes' with slogans like 'Vote for Cavendish and Cheetham'.[2]

The right to publish for a party was naturally worth a certain amount of money, and seems to have involved some obligations. The *Kentish Mercury* was denounced by the *West Kent Courier* for taking all the Conservative advertising it could get and then devoting very little space to politics and Conservative speeches. It would be unreasonable to conclude that the *Mercury* had been given the advertising in an unsuccessful attempt to buy its support, because by the time of the dissolution newspapers had committed themselves too far to be able to change sides, and in any case advertising was at times placed in hostile newspapers.[3]

Addresses sometimes mentioned benefits the candidate had brought to the constituency. The candidate could no longer affect an eighteenth-century independence of his constituents and he could not yet depend on party loyalty to

[1] This is the thesis of G. C. Thompson, *Public Opinion and Lord Beaconsfield 1875–1880* (London, 1886) and Henry Jephson, *The Platform* (London, 1892). Hartington, in 'Ten Liberal Speeches', B.M. 8139 6. 6. 12. On the intellectual difficulty of a mass meeting, see Gladstone to Granville, 2 Nov. 1878: P.R.O. 30–29–29.

[2] Nuffield Collection, particularly Cambridge and Elgin posters in folio vol. i; *New Mills and Hayfield Advertiser*, 9 Apr.

[3] *West Kent Courier*, 24 Apr.; Herbert Gladstone's advertisement in the *Globe*, 2 Apr.

cover his personal deficiencies. The wider issues of politics were the more normal topics of addresses; on the whole Conservatives more often referred to past events and Liberals more often referred to future legislation. To some extent the course of events encouraged parties to take these positions. The Conservatives looked back to the popular triumph of 'peace with honour' and had very few items of legislation to offer, while the Liberals felt that references to future domestic policy might win back those who, like *The Times*, approved of the government's handling of foreign affairs, but preferred the opposition's approach to finance and legislation.

Candidates, especially unopposed candidates, sometimes issued a formal address of goodwill with the comment that their views were well known to their constituents. However, candidates did not try to appeal to uncommitted voters by hinting that they were not really attached to their party, and they were not much more tolerant to pressure-groups which tried to push them out of the course they would normally have followed. They seem to have thought it was more useful to appeal to their allies than to try to conciliate their opponents, so that many Liberals declared for Local Option and many Conservatives declared against it. The address was important enough for candidates sometimes to receive help in drafting it. Before the important Buckinghamshire by-election of 1876 Granville drafted the address for the Liberal candidate. Leaders had no time to help in this way during the general election, but addresses still had to be acceptable to the election committee. There is no particular sign that the Caucuses or Hundreds of the National Liberal Federation were more inclined to give advice than the ordinary constituency committees which had no permanent existence.[1]

Public meetings, with a speech of forty minutes or an hour, were an important part of almost every candidate's campaign. Meetings were quieter and more decorous than they had been in the past. Perhaps because nomination on the hustings with the attendant rowdyism had ended, it was

[1] For a note on addresses, see Bibliography, p. 168. For Spencer, *Northampton Mercury*, 3 Apr.; for Buckinghamshire, Gladstone to Granville, 27 Aug. 1876: P.R.O. 30–29–29.

comparatively rare for candidates to have eggs and other missiles thrown at them. Hecklers tried to discomfort them, and while some speakers were able to crush them with a neat reply or bring them up to the platform and out-argue them, others were less successful; Sir William Forbes, Conservative candidate for West Aberdeenshire, was forced to admit that he knew very little about Bessarabia or about the Salisbury–Schouvaloff memorandum or, presumably, about the geographical effect of the policy it embodied.[1]

Most of the speeches read very like leading articles, perhaps because the politicians based themselves on the newspapers, or perhaps because the reporters thought they ought to sound like leading articles. Gladstone, Bright in his few appearances, Harcourt when his wit was not too forced, and occasionally Bradlaugh rose above this level. No Conservative speakers attained any very high level, for the speeches of Cross, Northcote, and Smith reached no more than a dignified mediocrity. One speech which fell below the accepted standard was picked out to embarrass the Conservatives: their candidate in North-West Lancashire, General Fielden, was selected at very short notice and he made a jerky and shapeless speech which looked politically illiterate. He probably did himself no good by confessing a little later that he had taken 'a stimulant' before the speech but as he gave an impression of honest though inarticulate patriotism he was elected at a time when no Conservative seat in Lancashire was really safe. From the comments on his performance he must have been below the general level of competence, but he was not unique. A little earlier there had been Lord Yarmouth, 'the stupidest fellow that ever lived—the only man that stood two contested elections and never opened his mouth'. The constituency was pretty certain to know if a candidate was a poor or a bashful speaker; whether this made any difference to the result is much harder to tell.[2]

The issues at stake did not make it hard for speakers to be comprehensible: the existing state of Europe was not much

[1] *Truth*, 1 Apr.; *The Scotsman*, 17 Mar.; *The Times*, 23 Mar.

[2] For Bradlaugh, *Northampton Mercury*, 21 Feb.; for Fielden, *Manchester Guardian*, 3, 8, and 10 Apr.; for Yarmouth, Beaconsfield to Lady Bradford, 6 Feb. 1879, Disraeli, *Letters to two Noble Ladies* (London, 1929), ii. 207.

discussed even by people who had a lot to say about the events of 1876 to 1878; economic orthodoxy, with its emphasis on a balanced Budget, was not too complicated; the legislation to be explained and defended was straightforward and untechnical. The work of administration did not take up much time, so that politicians could treat the work of explaining their policy in Parliament and in the country as their chief task. Winning elections was no longer a matter of arranging the representation of selected boroughs, so argument was becoming the only way for politicians to have a wide effect. One modern aid for speakers did exist: some candidates had speeches written for them. As there were no duplicated and circulated texts, reporters had to copy down every word, and this may have led to inaccuracy.[1]

Judging the course of public meetings does depend a great deal on the newspaper reporting, and this was not always good. Beaconsfield knew how widespread an effect his speeches outside Parliament could have: his Guildhall speeches of 1876 and 1877 had had a great influence on diplomacy and on public opinion during the Eastern crisis, and in the summer of 1879 he was in despair at the prospect of a City feast where he had 'to get up with a confused brain and an exhausted body, to make a speech every word of which will be criticized for months', presumably on the basis of newspaper reports. Accordingly, he was not pleased when his Aylesbury speech the following month was given 'two half-columns of incoherent rubbish' in *The Times*—even though he thought the other reports, especially the *Morning Post*, were satisfactory—and he called the habit of accepting *The Times*'s account as authentic 'an old but influential superstition'.[2]

Apart from possible inaccuracy, reporters did not say enough about the audiences' reactions to be very helpful guides. They preferred saying a hall was full or half-empty to estimating the numbers present, so it is not easy to find out how many people were exposed to speeches. The con-

[1] On speech-writing, Wright to Granville, 24 Aug. 1876: P.R.O. 30–29–26, and *The Scotsman*, 20 Mar. 1880.

[2] Beaconsfield to Lady Bradford, 6 Aug. and 19 Sept. 1879, Disraeli, op. cit. ii. 228 and 241. Gladstone had a higher opinion of *The Times*—see *Speeches in Scotland*, ii. 7.

centration on reporting the speeches rather than the popular reaction could be seen when Northcote spoke at Shoreditch. He was shouted down and could not get a hearing, an event which suggests that the government was less popular than had been thought. But instead of trying to find out why people were so annoyed the reporters valiantly tried to record what was said, and editorial comment was confined to protests that it was un-English not to give a man a fair hearing. About the only thing to attract a reporter's attention was the defeat of the vote of confidence in the candidate that was traditionally put and passed at the end of a meeting.[1]

Despite their inconveniences as sources of information for historians, newspapers gave the people of 1880 what they wanted. Lloyd George 'recalled tramping the fourteen miles to Portmadoc and back to get a London newspaper with a full report of one of Mr. Gladstone's speeches during the Midlothian campaign'. The walk was exceptional but the subsequent reading-aloud (by David's Uncle Richard) to an audience was quite usual. Verbatim reports of speeches were a response to public demand, and it was the best available way for voters to find out what politicians were thinking during the election.[2]

It has been suggested that the dominance of the London press over British political journalism was slighter than at any other period.[3] The power of serious newspapers was reduced by the 1867 Reform Bill which made it necessary to influence political parties rather than individual Members. By tacking from side to side Delane had contrived that *The Times* was on the winning side in 1868 and 1874 but in 1880 its position was very confused. Lord George Hamilton was too definite when he said that 1880 was the first election when *The Times* was not on the winning side, and so was *The Times*'s official history when it said Chenery, the editor, inclined to the Liberal side and Walter, the proprietor, to the Conservative. Trouble began when Delane failed to lay down a firm line on the Eastern Question. After he retired

---

[1] *The Times*, 24 and 25 Mar. Defeat of North Derbyshire vote of confidence in Conservative candidates, *New Mills and Hayfield Advertiser*, 2 Apr.

[2] Frank Owen, *Tempestuous Journey* (London, 1954), p. 32.

[3] Francis Williams, *Dangerous Estate* (London, 1956), p. 105.

in September 1877 the newspaper generally supported the government on foreign policy and the opposition on domestic policy. This was very much the position that Walter took up in his election address and it was not made any clearer by Walter's preference for Hartington as Prime Minister and his realization that Gladstone was inevitable. A few moderate Liberals may have been kept loyal to the party by this policy, but probably *The Times* itself would have been quite happy if it had avoided offending either side. A circulation of 50,000 was so small a fraction of the electorate that it was probably resigned to having very little direct influence on voters. Its power had to come from its direct impact on politicians rather than its effect on any large audience.[1]

The *Daily Telegraph* had a circulation of 250,000 and was outspoken, if not always consistent, in its attitude towards events. It had been a Liberal paper but had become pro-Turk—Labouchere said this was because the owner, Edward Lawson, had an uncle who held a large block of Turkish bonds[2]—and correspondingly anti-Gladstonian. It was a supporter of imperialism and may have done something to draw Liberals with imperialist views to the Conservative side. Its Conservatism was not yet very deep-rooted, for it showed every sign of being ready to desert to the Liberals when the result became clear.[3] The *Daily News* had a circulation of 170,000 and a high reputation for foreign news. It had been the first to report the Bulgarian atrocities, and had challenged the government's attitude to the press in India: it protested against Roberts's restrictions on reporting in Afghanistan, and it objected to the Vernacular Press Acts in India which gave the administration powers of censorship over all newspapers in the native languages of the inhabitants. The *Daily News* was a very firmly committed Liberal newspaper, and one of its services to the party was to call for unity loudly and frequently. The

---

[1] Lord George Hamilton, *Reminiscences and Reflections* (London, 1917), p. 28; *History of The Times*, ii. 507–8 and 521. *The Times*'s support for the government can be exaggerated: 'Two better articles than the first and third of yesterday I should not wish to read', Gladstone to Granville, 5 Jan. 1878: P.R.O. 30–29–29; *The Times*, 5 Apr.

[2] Hesketh Pearson, *Labby* (London, 1936), p. 134.

[3] *Daily Telegraph*, 3 Apr.

Conservatives accused it of trying to cement a coalition of irreconcilables; it might have been more reasonable to complain that the *News* did not define Liberal policy for fear of offending one group or another.[1]

Until 1874 these three papers, which between them dominated the London scene, had all been Liberal and the Conservative press had been outweighted. In 1880 the Liberals could rely on the *Daily News*, the newly launched *Daily Chronicle*, and the evening *Echo*, but had no other firm support in the daily press. On the Conservative side the *Standard* and the *Morning Post* may not have cared for imperialism and Tory Democracy, but they remained absolutely loyal.[2] Presumably most of their readers were enfranchised; on the Liberal side the mass-circulation Sunday papers, such as *Lloyd's Weekly News* and *Reynolds*, probably sold well among the unenfranchised. Their political comments were packed into the middle of interesting cases in court, but it would be misleading to compare them directly with the twentieth-century *News of the World*: they had strongly expressed political views and as they commanded a circulation that was not equalled until the days of Northcliffe they greatly strengthened the position of the Radicals in the London boroughs.[3]

At a more respectable level, the three most important weekly magazines supported the Liberals. *Punch* and the *Spectator* were more or less Gladstonian in their views, and *The Economist* devoted itself to reconciling the moderate Liberals to the main body of the party. The weighty monthly and quarterly magazines seem to have been fairly evenly balanced, and in any case it was unlikely that they would influence their readers very directly. Gladstone contributed to the magazines, and his view of what Liberal policy should be first appeared in the *Nineteenth Century*. Articles of this sort were intended to provide ammunition for other people, including journalists writing for daily papers, with which to appeal to the ordinary voter.[4]

[1] *Daily News*, 14 and 17 Feb.
[2] On the Liberal press, 'After', Nuffield Collection, folio vol. iii, on the *Standard*, see *Whitehall Review*, 14 Feb.
[3] 'A Tory View of the Election', *Nineteenth Century*, June 1880.
[4] 'The Country and the Government', ibid., Aug. 1879.

The Conservatives had expressed considerable satisfaction at the way the London daily press had supported
their foreign policy.[1] After the election, it must be noted,
their gratitude for this support diminished a little unreason-
ably. The results show that the Conservatives held their
ground better in the London and Home Counties area than
they did in the regions served by the provincial press. The
election may have been something of a triumph for the provincial press, but it was unfair to say 'the Conservative
party are formally represented in London by one evening
paper and informally by another, and partially by two
published in the morning'.[2] The *Standard* and the *Morning
Post* had given much more loyal support than this suggests.

This firmly Conservative author asserted that 'as a general
rule that title [independent] is assumed by the proprietors
of Liberal journals published in districts where the Conservative element is too strong for undiluted Radicalism to be
acceptable'. He offered a table, based on the papers' own
account of their position:

	England	Wales	Scotland	Ireland	The Islands	Total
Conservative	250	14	21	40	5	330
Liberal	316	29	78	51	8	472
Independent and neutral	429	21	60	47	7	564

and commented 'it is probably no exaggeration to say that
450 out of these 564 so-called Independent or Neutral
prints are distinctly allied to the Liberal Party, while in
three cases out of four they serve as mouthpieces of its more
advanced section'. The author suggested that the Conservatives had alienated newspapers by being less willing to
supply them with government information than the Liberals
had been. Other Conservatives suggested that Conservative
newspapers were too high-toned to make an impression, and
reading the Radical press was compared to moral dram-
drinking.[3]

---

[1] 'The Conservative Defeat', *Quarterly Review*, Apr. 1880.
[2] 'The Newspaper Press', ibid., Oct. 1880.
[3] 'Conservative Reorganisation', *Blackwood's Magazine*, June 1880; 'A Tory
View of the Election', *Nineteenth Century*, June 1880.

The provincial press did not in fact get advance information from governments. There were, as could be seen even in 1874, more Liberal voters than Conservative, and some proprietors may have followed rather than led their readers. Lastly, if the government was unpopular, newspapers would attack it: the Conservatives began at the wrong end by assuming that they were popular and that only partisan feeling could account for newspaper attacks. It has to be added that in many towns each party had a paper, and that in some cases the Conservative paper was the larger, or appeared daily, while the Liberal paper appeared weekly.[1] Newspapers may have shown too little concern about the difficulty of running a government but apart from this failing, not unique to 1880, reporting was reasonably fair and enormously long.

The newspapers did not look attractive; editors and proprietors were still thinking of a newspaper in terms of a book or a magazine.[2] Serious papers reserved the front page for advertisements; evening papers put editorial comment on it; only the popular Sunday papers put news there. Several columns, or even a whole page, in the centre of the paper were devoted to editorial comment. Newspapers, in London and in the provinces, were designed for a leisured class and had not yet begun to search for mass-circulation at the cost of serious political influence. The emphasis on what was said rather than what was done made it hard to find what the electorate was thinking. The short notes from the constituencies, published as 'Election Intelligence', mentioned manœuvres within local party organizations, but this was still politics at the level of people who were closely concerned with it. Editorial writers occasionally tried to estimate public opinion, though of course their main purpose was to state the case for one party forcefully and several times over; they were excited and sometimes violent, and this makes it uncertain that their estimates were intended as more than party propaganda. The *Morning Post* predicted on 22 March that the Conservatives would gain seven seats

---

[1] Thus, Exeter had the weekly Liberal *Devon Weekly Times* and the daily Conservative *Exeter and Plymouth Gazette*.

[2] J. Robertson-Scott, *Life and Death of a Newspaper* (London, 1952), p. 76.

in the London and Middlesex area; in the event they lost
three. It is true that the *Morning Post* had previously said
that people had already decided which way they would vote,
but it seems quite possible that its prediction was primarily
designed to raise Conservative spirits and this has to be
allowed for in reading public statements of Conservative
optimism.[1]

Several pages in *The Times*, and two or three pages in the
other London papers, were devoted to reports of speeches.
Important statesmen appeared verbatim, and lesser speakers
were scaled down according to their political standing.
Gladstone made altogether exceptional demands on space,
and as his speeches spread from one page into a second,
complaints began to be heard about his volubility.[2] Local
papers reported their own party's candidates in the district
at length, but were less concerned than the London papers
about reporting political opponents; they also carried short
reports of the major politicians. The provincial papers like
the *Manchester Guardian* and the *Leeds Mercury* observed
the same conventions as the London papers. As a result of
this extensive reporting, reinforced by the party organizations which concentrated their publishing energies on bringing out speeches by party leaders as pamphlets, the electorate
had an opportunity to find out in great detail about the
position of the parties' spokesmen, though the structure of
the political parties meant that they were not presented with
definitive statements of party policy.

Few speeches read as well as they sound, but the platform
oratory of the time was somewhat literary in form, and the
existence of volumes of sermons and the practice of reading
aloud had given Victorian audiences a good training for
following speeches from the printed text. None of the
authors of pamphlets showed a particular talent for the
written word—*Bulgarian Horrors* is clearly the work of a
great orator, not a great writer—and probably the dominance
of pamphlets based on speeches meant that other authors

---

[1] *Morning Post*, 12 Mar.; Beaconsfield, it must be remembered, was cheerful even
in private letters.
[2] *The Times*, 18 Mar. Speech of Lord George Hamilton, 'Present Position of the
Conservative Party', Conservative Central Office pamphlets.

wrote in the same way.[1] Neither party maintained a research department, and they ignored the advantages which print could bring. Pamphlets could have provided maps with which to follow the course of the Eastern crisis, because newspapers produced them infrequently and of course did not publish them just to illustrate politicians' speeches. This meant that arguments about diplomatic policy had to be carried on in fairly general terms if the audience was not to be out of its depth. The newspaper proprietors themselves might have benefited from studying maps: in the *Lawson* v. *Labouchere* trial for criminal libel it became clear that Lawson knew very little about the geography of the areas about which his newspaper, the *Daily Telegraph*, had advised the government so forcefully.[2]

Diagrams might have been as helpful for discussing financial policy as maps for discussing foreign policy, but they were used equally rarely.[3] In financial affairs even a printed text could be a better guide than a speech: figures handled on a platform were inevitably incomplete because an audience was unlikely to listen to anything more than a simplified version of the complexities of revenue statistics year by year. Both sides produced pamphlets on the subject, marshalling the facts in different ways: the Conservatives talked about the total amount of income-tax imposed in the five years of Conservative rule and the five previous years of Liberal rule, and the Liberals pointed out that under Lowe the income-tax had fallen Budget by Budget and under Northcote it had gone up Budget by Budget. The Liberals complained of the rising cost of government and the Conservatives replied that the population had increased and that many new items of expenditure, such as the money spent on education, were the result of Liberal legislation.[4]

There were legitimate party debating points, but the

---

[1] It was said at the conference of the National Union that the tongue had outweighed the pen. *Minutes of the 1880 Conference of the National Union.*

[2] Salisbury's 'Despatch of April 1, 1878' was published as a pamphlet with a map. Conservative Central Office pamphlets: Pearson, op. cit., pp. 151–2.

[3] An example in 'A Political Handbook for the People'. B.M. 8139 aaa 5.

[4] 'Taxation under Tory and Liberal Governments' and 'Liberal and Conservative Finance,' National Liberal Club pamphlets, vols. 321 and 315; 'Conservative Finance and Liberal Fallacies', *National Union Pamphlet*, no. 39; 'A Few Words on the Finances', Conservative Central Office pamphlets.

longer pamphlets do not seem to have had a clearly defined audience in mind. Few pamphlets were designed as speakers' handbooks; on the other hand, the quantities of information provided in the more serious pamphlets must have been very heavy reading for anyone not closely involved in politics. It is possible to extract a reasonably unbiased account of the situation by reading them carefully, but that is not enough for good propaganda.[1] The more pre-digested approach of shorter pamphlets like 'Why I'll vote Liberal' was probably more effective. This pamphlet included a section giving fifty reasons for voting Liberal; one was that Liberal policies helped trade 'while the Conservatives, by a bad policy, make bad times worse'. This catchphrase seems to have been so effective that it was used again in 1885—Ostrogorski noticed it, with some irritation, and condemned it as a piece of illogical thinking. But while it was inappropriate in 1885, it seems to have been effective in 1880,[2] and it was certainly a clear and easily comprehensible argument.

There do not seem to have been many short and serious pamphlets, but several of those written in a lighter manner hit quite effectively at weak points in the opposing party. The lives of Gladstone and Beaconsfield were told in coloured booklets. A black-and-white Conservative booklet called 'Liberal Misleaders' gave short and unfavourable biographical details of a number of Liberal leaders, with portraits and extracts from the attacks on their colleagues that could be found in their speeches.[3] The Gladstonians published a number of pamphlets in the form of fables about Ben or Beaky the dishonest hotelier or bailiff, with their hero as the honest old retainer ready to take up his old job when the need was recognized. There were a few anti-Gladstone fables; Hartington and Granville were ignored by both sides. The story of the Eastern crisis could be told as a tale of the bailiff tricking two of his neighbours and annoying some of the others. References to the prodigality of his estate-management or to the gimcrack splendour of his

---

[1] See 'Farmers' Grievances', National Liberal Club pamphlets, vol. 6110; 'The Policy of the Government on the Eastern Question', *National Union Pamphlet*, no. 33.

[2] Nuffield Collection, octavo vol. iii; Ostrogorski, op. cit. i. 407.

[3] Nuffield Collection, quarto vol.

hotel, reminded people that the story had personal consequences for them.[1] Foreign policy was easier to tell as a story
than any other issue in the campaign, and the story could be
told in cartoons like the series about the doctor who pro-
fessed great concern about the integrity of Turkey and then
set out to cure her ailments by cutting off her arms and
legs.[2]

A great deal of use was made of these less serious publi-
cations. 'Ben changes the Motto' had a sale of 25,000:[3]
probably a good number of these copies were bought in
bulk by staunch party supporters and given away to less
committed voters, but it is worth noting that while the
serious pamphlets issued by the party organizations often
announce a retail price and a price for a bulk purchase of a
hundred or so, the less serious pamphlets usually just give
the retail price, which suggests they were to be sold com-
mercially. A non-partisan booklet like 'The Grand National
Steeplechase' must have been published as a commercial
undertaking, and if there was a market for such booklets
there was probably a market for more partisan, but equally
light, pamphlets among people who wanted to learn about
politics in an easy way. These people would have found it
easier to learn the Liberal case; the two parties were fairly
evenly matched in serious pamphleteering but the Conservatives seem to have had difficulty in finding humorous
writers.

Songs and ballads were produced during the campaign,
and after the election there were a number of songs to celebrate the defeat of Beaconsfield and the return of Gladstone.
They do not look easy to sing; the meetings of the Radical
candidates in Northampton ended with a song whose first
line was 'Return Bradlaugh and Labouchere'.[4] The songs
were written to be sung to popular tunes, the name of the
tune printed with the text of the song. In Bolton at least
eleven Conservative songs were printed, referring more or
less closely to events in the town. One of them blamed J. K.

---

[1] Nuffield Collection, octavo vols. 'Ben changes the Motto', 'Squire Bull and his
Bailiff Benjamin', 'How Ben behaved Himself', 'My Neighbour'. 'Churchwarden
Gledstanes' is a Conservative fable.

[2] Ibid., quarto vol.   [3] *Truth*, 19 Feb.

[4] *Northampton Mercury*, 3 Apr.

Cross, the sitting Liberal Member, for poor trade: unless this was a reference to a local event in which Cross seemed to have intensified the depression, it was ill judged, because if people were going to blame politicians for the depression they were going to blame the government. Another song reminded voters of the torchlight procession—an American form of political demonstration that did not occur in British elections very often.[1]

Other songs in Bolton denounced Gladstone and Derby for Radicalism, and personal attacks like this are a useful reminder that the election was not going to be won by argument alone. The posters showed this clearly and crudely. They varied from rough black-and-white drawings to long printed messages. Short incisive slogans, apart from the Liberals' unchanging affirmation of 'Peace, Retrenchment and Reform', seem not to have been used.[2] The designers seem to have been possessed by a desire to get everything into a single poster without caring much about a simple design that was easy to follow. A few posters, such as the picture of Gladstone the Woodman about to chop down Beaconsfield the Upas-Tree, were put up in several towns, and a great many others had no specific reference to a particular constituency: anti-flogging posters appeared in several places and do not look as if they came from a central organization.[3] Neither the National Union nor the National Liberal Federation seem to have spent money on posters, and it was unlikely that any other central organization would pay for them; some of the money spent on posters was for paying people to put them up, which could slip into bribery.[4] The concentration on pamphlets of the Federation and the Union may have been the result of a feeling that their duty as organizations was mainly

[1] Nuffield Collection, quarto vol. For processions, see also Watkin Williams to Gladstone, 24 Mar.: Add. MSS. 44462, ff. 265–6, and *The Times*, 6 Apr.

[2] In his second speech on 26 Nov. 1879 Gladstone commented that a banner inscribed 'Peace, Retrenchment and Reform' was decorating the hall. Simon's address, and use in Westminster, *The Times*, 15 and 26 Mar.

[3] Unless otherwise mentioned, comments on posters are based on the Nuffield Collection; letter in the *Daily Telegraph*, 12 May, on the anti-flogging posters.

[4] No posters were put up in the City; the two sides reckoned to save themselves £18,000 by this: *World*, 27 Mar. The South Essex Liberals thought their opponents paid a lot for poster-sites: *Daily News*, 2 Apr.

educational; the Conservatives put out one pamphlet of questions, quotations, and short arguments, each page of which could be used as a poster, though a poster with a rather complicated message.[1]

On the other hand, many posters were designed for local contests, sometimes just showing the candidate's face or name, but sometimes by referring to local policy and local conditions. Even within local struggles there was more self-assertion and self-encouragement than discussion of policy. Designers of posters thought it was more useful to show their candidate winning the race than to argue a case or drive home a favourable point. In Newcastle, for instance, posters took it for granted that Joseph Cowen, the sitting Radical imperialist, could decide whether the second Member was to be the Liberal candidate Ashton Dilke or the sitting Tory Member, Hamond. The rivals for second place concentrated on saying that they were closer to Cowen, without discussing policy issues which would justify the claim.

Most posters had pictures, but the 'Tory Catechism' and a number of election addresses appeared as lengthy printed messages, and so did the Home Rule Committee's appeal to all Irishmen to vote against Benjamin Disraeli. 'The Liberal Circus', a variety turn compered by Hartington, Gladstone, and Parnell was a satirical poster with no illustration. The Home Rule Committee preferred green paper, but most printed posters were on white paper, in the party colour which varied confusingly from constituency to constituency but in general Conservative meant blue and Liberal yellow.[2] Whether the allegorical pictures added very much, except for the few voters who could not read, is doubtful;[3] they were almost all transpositions into pictures of an idea that had originally been thought of in verbal terms.

A few posters contained personal insults. Posters referred to Beaconsfield's Jewish origins, and a Conservative poster of Gladstone talking with the 'sh's' of the East End Jew probably recoiled on Beaconsfield. At a more responsible level, when Lowe referred to Beaconfield's handling of

---

[1] Nos. 4, 8, 10, 11, 12, 14, 17, 22, 27, 28, 30, 32, 33, 35 are in Nuffield Collection folio volumes.

[2] *Globe*, 31 Mar.   [3] *The Times*, 13 Mar.

English 'which is, after all, his native language', *The Times* was quick to denounce this flash of anti-Semitism. There were a few pictures of Conservative depression contrasted with the sunshine of Liberal prosperity, and others of Conservative prestige and glory. These image-creating posters seem to have been less frequent than those which presented an argument, and the latter were in turn used less often than posters which in effect said 'We Will Win'.

The assumption implicit in the long speeches and the extensive reporting was that arguments would decide the issue, and statesmen were coming to feel that it was their duty to carry on, outside as well as inside Parliament, a perpetual debate. The debate rested on the convention that the result of the election was decided by the rational choice of millions of voters, who were unmoved by fear, favour, or prejudice. This convention had healthy effects: it helped considerably in the elimination of corrupt practices during the nineteenth century and it meant that politicians had to be reasonable in putting forward their programmes. Of course, speeches and addresses were not decisive, and probably no politician imagined that argument by itself would win an election. A very large number of people were immovably committed by prejudice, personal interest, or religious background to one party or the other. The Ballot, extension of the franchise, and limitation of expenses reduced the power of illegitimate influences, but not even their complete elimination would make the election entirely rational—one obvious difference between 1874 and 1880 was that more people voted in 1880, and it is statistically possible that the difference in the results were entirely due to the people who had not voted in 1874 and were not normally at all interested in politics.

Though the shift of votes was probably less irrational than that, non-logical influences must have been important. The Conservatives may have gained ground in 1874 because they could spend more freely, but the Liberals seem to have been at no serious financial disadvantage in 1880. People felt the other side should be given a chance, and this feeling was reinforced by the depression in trade: the voters might not be able to prove that the government caused the depression, but it did not help the government.[1] Motives of this sort were understandable, but they did not make for the perfectly logical discussion that was demanded by some of the electoral conventions. The considerations must not be exaggerated: the vote was still the prized possession of men of substance and while there was no reason to assume that they were more disinterested than the rest of the population, a large proportion of them—perhaps a larger proportion than in any subsequent election—had the leisure that goes with a substantial number of servants, and could study the question at some length. There seems to have been little danger that audiences would dwindle, or that interest would decline, when candidates discussed the issues seriously.

[1] Editorial in *The Times*, 5 Apr.; long article in the *Standard*, 8 Apr. Bath to Granville, 19 Apr., 'I confess to a feeling, unreasonable perhaps . . . that the material condition of the country will improve': P.R.O. 30–29–27.

V

BRIBERY, CORRUPTION, AND
ALL THAT

No mention was made, when discussing the methods used to communicate political arguments, of canvassing. It was the oldest technique of getting in touch with the voters, for it dated from a time before newspapers and public meetings. All too often it revealed its origins by appearing in a form that showed it had once been the method by which a landlord, or a man with some other sort of power, made his views known to the people whose obedience he could count on. Shortly after the election three Radicals, Cohen, Dillwyn, and Morgan Lloyd, introduced a Bill to make all canvassing a corrupt practice.[1] They believed canvassing would destroy the good work of the Ballot Act, because a canvasser would be bound to form some impression of the way a man would vote and this opened the door to corruption and intimidation.[2]

Canvassing was just one way in which the election fell away from the high ideal of voters listening to arguments for and against the government in speeches and newspaper articles and then deciding on logical grounds how they would vote. Rhetorical exaggeration in speech-making was something of a deviation from the purest austerity of rational argument, but this chapter is concerned with what happened when money, influence, or brute strength affected votes more than argument on the main issues did. Many people canvassed very honestly without any thought of gain or any offer to give a bribe, but an enthusiastic request for a vote is

[1] *Morning Post*, 1 June. For opposition to organized canvassing, see also Buxton's pamphlet 'Electoral Purity and Economy'. B.M. 8138 cc 8(g).

[2] Canvassers' figures were not necessarily correct. Gladstone was told he would win in Midlothian by 1781 votes to 1144. Agent to Gladstone, 14 Feb.: Add. MSS. 44462, f. 90. The actual figures were 1579 to 1368. Before his first visit to Midlothian, a majority of 196 had been forecast. W. Saunders, *The New Parliament of 1880* (London, 1880), p. 245.

not the same as a logical argument, and it is easy to see why Radicals who believed that argument should prevail were opposed to canvassing.

Apart from this, canvassing could lead to corrupt practices. Canvassers were sometimes paid, and it was suggested that as a paid canvasser did not work very hard, the chief use of paying him was to buy his vote.[1] Candidates might have employed paid canvassers in order to escape the risk of dependence on a body of unpaid political enthusiasts like the Liberal Hundreds, but there is very little sign that they did hire canvassers in order to carry on an independent line of policy. The independent Liberals like Cowen and Sir Edward Watkin, who survived although they supported the government's foreign policy, had a good deal of local influence as well as money. Canvassers were undoubtedly necessary, and if they were to be obtained in the numbers needed in a large constituency it could only be done by paying for them or by appealing to party loyalty and enthusiasm.[2]

Naturally candidates tried to call on the electors personally, though a few addresses contained confessions that the constituency was so large that this was impossible. A personal visit by the candidate, or by a member of his committee, meant that the elector was exposed to the sort of pressure that a member of the upper classes can inevitably exert over his inferiors in a deferential society. Canvassers did not trust to deference alone, and made a point of calling on people on whom they had some influence.[3] This was far enough removed from the ideal of every voter making up his own mind for some conscientious candidates to refrain from canvassing. In the first place the candidate could not put his views forward any more clearly by canvassing than by speeches in public. In the second place canvassing by social superiors led naturally to what Gladstone, a little unfairly,

[1] *Globe*, 22 Mar.
[2] The Marylebone Conservatives employed 100 canvassers apart from volunteers: *Morning Post*, 30 Mar. In Westminster the Liberals had 150 paid and 200 unpaid workers: *Daily News*, 1 Apr. For a volunteer canvasser, see de Lisle to Gladstone, 13 Mar.: Add. MSS. 44462, ff. 184–7. See also R. T. McKenzie, *British Political Parties* (London, 1955), pp. 164–5. It was said that, without canvassers, very few people would vote in large towns: *Manchester Guardian*, 5 Feb.
[3] 'Tamson's Vote', Nuffield Collection, octavo vol. iii.

described as a voter 'suffering himself to be wheedled by his own free choice or his own inattention'. Gladstone went on to say: 'A man has only himself to thank if that liberty [of secret voting] is lost, and . . . I have no remedy to supply by which his want of courage and manhood can be made good.'[1] However, perhaps as a result of a closer study of the facts of the situation in Midlothian be reminded an audience a little later of the way that Sir Walter Scott had denied the authorship of the Waverley Novels.[2] This example was widely followed; after the election the Conservatives said '250 of those who had voluntarily undertaken to vote for Lord Dalkeith voted for Mr. Gladstone.'[3] No doubt some of those people had been converted by Gladstone's speeches and perhaps the canvassers' figures were on the optimistic side, but it is obvious that some people had been bullied into promising to vote for Dalkeith. There were a number of other complaints from candidates who polled decidedly fewer votes than they had been promised, and some of these promises may have been obtained by undue pressure; the Conservative candidate in North Durham felt very aggrieved because although 6,000 of the 6,300 people who had promised to vote for him appeared at the polls, only 5,000 of them voted for him.[4] These complaints that voters were breaking promises given to canvassers were really based on a feeling that the Ballot Act should not have been passed.

Some candidates accordingly declined to canvass, just as men of great distinction like Mill and Macaulay had declined to canvass in the past; this did not prevent their supporters from canvassing for them. Other candidates declined to take advantage of the laws permitting them to convey voters to the polling-stations, or announced that they would rely on subscriptions for their expenses.[5] These candidates did quite well, which suggests that the electorate was in the

[1] Speech of 24 Mar., *Speeches in Scotland*, ii. 51.

[2] *Manchester Guardian*, 30 Mar. and 2 Apr. A man wrote to *The Times*, 3 Apr., to point out that a voter could always give up the wrong ticket at the polling station, if he had been given a polling-card.

[3] 'The Reign of Bunkum', *Blackwood's Magazine*, May 1880; *Spectator*, 24 Apr.

[4] *East Suffolk Gazette*, 13 Apr.; Douglas-Pennant's speech in *Daily News*, 14 Apr.; *Hereford Journal*, 1 May. For Durham, see *Durham Chronicle*, 16 Apr.

[5] *Hereford Times*, 3 and 10 Apr.; *Daily News*, 30 Apr.; A. W. Humphrey, *A History of Labour Representation* (London, 1912), p. 88.

mood for stricter regulation of elections. Candidates who stuck to canvassing and made no public speeches were looked down on and risked being accused of conducting their campaigns on a basis of bribery. When Sir Robert Carden fought the Barnstaple by-election, early in 1880, without making any speeches, the Liberals referred to the 'shower of gold' that accompanied him. At the general election Johnson, the Liberal candidate for Exeter, confessed that he was a businessman and no speaker, and he set about intensive canvassing. The Conservatives asked why he did not stick to his business, and they called him the 'breeches-pocket candidate'.[1]

If candidates tried to win votes by means that had nothing to do with the issues, some electors chose to disregard the question of foreign policy and finance that were accepted by government and opposition as the major issues, and tried to force their views on other issues upon the candidates; this activity by pressure-groups was rather different from the tentative efforts of the party organizations to force their views on major issues upon dissident candidates. The constitutionally orthodox and respectable position about people who tried to force candidates to commit themselves on minor issues was expressed by Gladstone, commenting on a letter from a Midlothian Liberal who said he would have to stand neutral because Gladstone had not supported Sir Wilfred Lawson's Temperance motion. Gladstone said he could not believe any Liberal would say:

> Though I think the government has mismanaged domestic affairs, though I think the government has disparaged and lowered the character of the Empire in foreign affairs, though I think it has laden us with the responsibility of needless and therefore guilty wars, yet I will help to cure none of these things; but because I cannot get my abstract resolution I will remain neutral.[2]

But however unreasonable such behaviour may have been, groups did ask candidates for pledges on particular issues. It is convenient to consider all these groups as pressure-groups, though some of the largest of them resembled loosely attached sections of a political party almost as much

[1] *Devon Weekly Times*, 30 Jan.; Exeter and Plymouth Gazette, 18 Mar.
[2] Speech of 19 Mar., *Speeches in Scotland*, ii. 39.

as the modern pressure-groups designed for lobbying. Disestablishment, Home Rule, and Local Option, the main issues on which pledges were asked, were compatible with the principles of the Liberal party; the Liberation Society, the Home Rule Confederation, and temperance societies like the Blue Ribbon Club and the Order of Good Templars were all predominantly Liberal in inclination; and the opponents of these measures, the Church Defence Institution, the Orange Order (which operated in Lancashire as well as in Ulster), and the Licensed Victuallers' Association tended to support the Conservative party. The pro-Liberal organizations had the harder job, because they had to persuade candidates to commit themselves to a change in the law, while it was enough for the pro-Conservative organizations if they could persuade candidates that a change was not appropriate at that moment, or that the issue was not yet one on which people had to make up their minds. The forces of inertia, and all the influences that help maintain party unity, were on the side of the pro-Conservative organizations and against the pro-Liberal organizations, which were denounced as 'crochet-mongers'. Nevertheless 'crochet-mongers' had some success, and might have had more if they could have shown that they really controlled the votes of their followers.[1]

It was at one time thought that the tactical strength of a mobilized pressure-group was demonstrated by Parnell's instructions, during the 1885 election, that Irishmen living in England should vote Conservative. It is still accepted that a large number of Irishmen voted Conservative in 1885, but they seem to have done so for religious reasons, because they thought Chamberlain's 'Free Schools' would harm the position of Catholic Schools.[2] Except in conditions like this, the

---

[1] Chapter 10 of Saunders, op. cit., is called 'Crochets'. See also M. Ostrogorski, *Democracy and Political Parties* (London, 1902), pp. 563–7; J. Chamberlain, 'The Next Page of the Liberal Programme', *Fortnightly Review*, Oct. 1874; *The Economist*, 14 Feb.; Birmingham Good Templars, *Morning Post*, 12 Mar.; addresses by the Church Association, the Church Defence Institution, and the Licensed Victuallers' Association, *The Times*, 17 Mar. It must be remembered that these groups were powerful only because they represented powerful interests: brewers and publicans would have been important whether there was a Licensed Victuallers' Association or not.

[2] C. H. D. Howard, 'The Parnell Manifesto of November 21', *English Historical*

supporters of the large pressure groups were in fact committed to one party or the other. If they became dissatisfied
with the party they had been supporting they could sulk, as
the nonconformists sulked in 1874, but they could hardly
join the other side. By sulking they reminded the party
leaders not to take their support for granted, and thus they
created the classic problem for a party leader: how is he to
keep up the enthusiasm of the section among the party
zealots which is more extreme than the party as a whole, and
at the same time avoid frightening away potential supporters?

The problem was not as bad as it might have been for the
Liberals in 1880, because the three large topics of the pressure-groups were not prominent. Gladstone praised the
helpfulness of the nonconformists for not making Disestablishment an issue, the Home Rulers were content to
turn the Conservatives out, and Local Option was put on
one side by asking for details of the proposals for compensation. Compensation for depriving publicans of the right to
sell liquor was a respectable principle; it reassured the
publicans and it reminded people that even if they obtained
the right to close public-houses by a local plebiscite, they
would have to pay for exercising the right.[1] The absence of
strong pressure on these three issues may have reduced the
enthusiasm of the pro-Conservative groups, who had
nothing immediate to worry about. Some Conservatives
announced that they were in favour of the Established
Church and a few Liberals committed themselves to Disestablishment; most Liberals committed themselves to
support the Burials Act and left the issue of Disestablishment alone.[2]

A new pressure-group, the Farmers' Alliance, also looked
like a loosely attached section of the Liberal party. Its programme was accepted by about sixty candidates, of whom all
but two or three were Liberals, and its magazine, the *Mark*

Review, lxii (1947); C. C. O'Brien, *Parnell and his Party* (London, 1957), p. 116.
The Irish realized the advantages they might gain if they held the balance of power
in 1880. Posters in Nuffield Collection, folio vols. ii and iii.

[1] Gladstone's speeches of 26 Nov. 1879, and 19 Mar., *Speeches in Scotland*, i. 38
and ii. 38; *The Times*, 13 Mar.; W. Saunders, op. cit., pl 183.

[2] 'A Nonconformist on the Election', *Nineteenth Century*, Apr. 1880; 'The
Conservative Defeat', *Quarterly Review*, Apr. 1880.

Lane Express, advised readers to vote Liberal in an editorial on 22 March. The Alliance had a set of questions for candidates, and the anti-landlord bias of the questions made them more acceptable to Liberals than to Conservatives.[1] So far as there was a Conservative counter-organization it was the Chamber of Agriculture, which had a programme accepted by about forty of the more pro-tenant farmer of the Conservative candidates.[2] Landlords could, in the normal course of social life, meet to work out their responses to any tenants' revolt that might be threatening. The depression of the late seventies was so severe that it led farmers to ask if their interests were as identical with their landlords' interests as they were told by Tory newspapers, Tory parsons, and Tory squires. It is not necessary to accept the landlords' claim that their tenants were being alienated from them by political agitators.[3] Bad weather and bad harvests had encouraged the Alliance, the landlords took no interest in it and so had no chance of preventing it from becoming a pro-Liberal organization.

Apart from these large pressure-groups, there were several others that looked rather more like pressure-groups of the present day in the sense that they were free from commitment to a party. The small shopkeepers had a Traders' Defence Association which can be taken as an example. It asked candidates to pledge themselves to do something to check co-operative stores. The original (Rochdale) co-operative stores do not seem to have been the target of attack; the complaints were about organizations like the Civil Service Stores which were open to the attack that it was unfair, and bad for the nation's affairs, that men should draw one salary as civil servants and another salary for organizing the stores during office hours. After the election it was admitted that the shopkeepers' lobbying of candidates had had very little effect, but during the campaign rather more had been expected. Candidates were guardedly favourable to the shopkeepers, but tried to avoid pledges. The

[1] *The Times*, 17 Mar.; *Mark Lane Express*, 22 Mar., 5 and 19 Apr.; *Spectator*, 24 Apr.

[2] *Mark Lane Express*, 5 Apr.; *Exeter and Plymouth Gazette*, 28 Apr.

[3] 'Who are the Farmers' Friends', *National Union Pamphlet*, no. 64; T. G. Rigg, *Political Parties, Positions and Prospects* (London, 1881), p. 94.

co-operative stores were quite popular: the Buckinghamshire shopkeepers noticed with great distaste that as soon as
Beaconsfield became a peer and stopped needing their votes
he gave up patronizing the local shops and bought from the
stores and had things sent down from London. If this feeling
was at all widespread, candidates might hesitate to offend a
relatively large number of co-operative stores customers for
the sake of the shopkeeper vote.[1] Two 'health' pressure-
groups can be noted because of the different approaches
they took. The opponents of compulsory vaccination concentrated on asking candidates for pledges and in one or
two constituencies the anti-vaccinationist voters turned the
balance. The opponents of the Contagious Diseases Act,
which provided for compulsory medical inspection of
prostitutes and suspected prostitutes in garrison towns, did
ask for support at the election, but concentrated on lobbying
in the Commons. In 1886 their agitation succeeded, and the
legislation was repealed.[2]

The Trade Unions, which had been active in 1868 and
1874, did much less in 1880. The cycle of agitation and
legislation which began with the 1867 Royal Commission
on Trade Unions ended with the 1875 Act. There was no
sign that gratitude for this measure weakened the Trade
Unions' normal attachment to the Liberal Party. Burt and
Macdonald were re-elected, Broadhurst was elected for the
first time, and a few others like Lucraft and Joseph Arch also
stood. All of them were Liberals, although one or two of
them stood against official Liberal candidates which may
have helped the Conservatives. The men who stood against
official candidates were nevertheless Liberals: Gladstone was
able to persuade Newton, a working man's candidate, not
to stand in Greenwich and he devoted part of his speech of

[1] Policy statement of the Traders' Defence Association, *Morning Post*, 15 Mar.
Pro-retail traders speeches of Morley and Grant, *The Times*, 22 Mar.; pro-customer
letters, ibid., 27 Mar. and 3 Apr. See also ibid., 23 and 24 Mar., and 10 Apr.;
Surrey Comet, 4 Mar.; *Exeter and Plymouth Gazette*, 12 and 17 Mar. For Beaconsfield's shopping, G. W. E. Russell, *Portraits of the Seventies* (London, 1916), p. 43.

[2] Gladstone's speech of 12 Mar., in *The Times*, 13 Mar. *Manchester Guardian*,
23 Mar. *Cambridge Express*, 17 Apr. For other pressure-groups: Anti-Game Law
League, *Winchester Observer*, 31 Jan.; and Central Sunday Closing Association,
Church of England Working Men's Society, and Patriotic Association, all in
Morning Post, 20 Mar.

12 March to discouraging the Marxist H. M. Hyndman from standing in Marylebone and splitting the Liberal vote. 'Labour' candidates were all Liberals and it was taken for granted that if they stood they would obtain votes that would otherwise go to the Liberals.[1]

Because of the 1875 Act or because of the depression most trade unionists did not ask candidates for pledges. The railway workers were an exception. They wanted a change in the law of common employment which at that time laid down that a worker injured by the negligence of another employee of the company had no claim against the company. As railway companies were large and railway work was dangerous, railway employees suffered more than most people from the way the law worked. The Liberal brewer Bass, Member for Derby, which had a large railway-workers' vote, encouraged the pressure for changing the law and so did the Liberal railway-director Members Brassey, MacIver, and Watkin. Perhaps because there had been some alarm about the number of railway accidents in the previous five years, there was no very strong opposition from other directors. A Government Bill, framed to meet the needs of the railwaymen, was introduced early in the new Parliament and the Fourth Party amused itself by making the Bill more radical and extending it to meet the needs of other trades.[2]

To the extent that the change was brought about by lobbying, the work was done by the Amalgamated Society of Railway Servants. The Society had enrolled only 14,000 out of the 300,000 railway workers and dependants, but it was presumably representative of the feelings of most of the others. Its magazine, the *Railway Service Gazette*, proclaimed in an editorial that appeared in three successive issues, 'The political power of the railway servants is so great that the contending political parties must bid for it'. The *Gazette* was encouraged in this belief by the sight of

[1] Humphrey, op. cit., pp. 86–87. *Morning Post*, 18 Mar.
[2] The main source is the *Railway Service Gazette*, the A.S.R.S's weekly newspaper. The law had been established in *Priestley* v. *Fowler* (1837). See also Salisbury to Beaconsfield, 16 Jan. 1875: Christ Church Papers; H. Gorst, *The Fourth Party* (London, 1906), p. 89. The railwaymen's vote was considered an important factor in the Buckinghamshire by-election. Carrington to Granville: P.R.O. 30–29–26.

Raikes, a Conservative Member, producing a resolution in support of the railwaymen's case before the dissolution; it noted that three or four hundred of his six thousand constituents at Chester were railwaymen. In its editorial encouraging railwaymen to make the parties bid for their votes, the *Gazette* pointed to the example of the Licensed Victuallers, the teetotallers, and the nonconformists. Like the organizations it sent questions to candidates and published notes on the replies. Apart from about 20 committed supporters who were not asked, 175 candidates gave favourable answers. Most of them were Liberals, though in towns like York with a strong railwaymen's vote all the candidates were in favour of changing the law.[1] The same was true at Sheffield, a railway centre important enough for the *Gazette* to bring out one of its special numbers, in which a page or two was reset to discuss the position in a particular constituency—special numbers were brought out for North Nottingham and East Retford in which the Liberal candidates were recommended. Somebody in Sheffield persuaded the editor that Waddy, the Liberal Member who had just left his seat at Barnstaple to go there, was planning to move to yet another constituency and the editor agreed to a Sheffield special number recommending Mundella and the Conservative candidate Stuart Wortley. But Waddy was not moving to another constituency, and the pro-Waddy Travelling Secretary of the Amalgamated Society was furious at being thrown over in this way. The railwaymen's vote and the influence of the *Gazette* may not often have been decisive, but as Waddy lost by only forty votes the manipulation of the *Gazette* was probably the last straw that broke his back.[2]

The doubtful power of the Railway Servants can be contrasted with the assured position of the railway interest. Many Members of the new Parliament, just like many Members of the old Parliament, were directors or employers and owed some of their position to their influence over their employees. Brighton, Hythe, and Sandwich were centres of railway power. The Liberals lost Maidstone partly as the

[1] Debate of 9 Mar., *Railway Service Gazette*, 5 and 26 Mar., 2 and 9 Apr.
[2] Ibid., 20 Mar., 16 and 23 Apr.

result of a railway director's influence. The Conservatives lost Brecon as a result of money and the railway 'screw'.[1] At Plymouth MacIver, who was President of the Railway Servants, gained a seat for the Liberals. Further north the directors' influence was smaller; like other industrialists they told their workers how they wanted them to vote, but this was not so effective in towns where the railway company was not the only employer. Industrialists, like their workers, were usually Liberals; railway directors were more evenly balanced between the parties perhaps because they sometimes owed their position on a Board to their position as landlords. Neither industrialists nor railway directors had any special interest to press for in 1880.[2]

The analogy between the industrialists' electoral power and that of the landlord can be taken too far. In a constituency dominated by a single large industrial establishment the proprietor could probably guarantee his own return. Whether he could treat it as a pocket borough and guarantee someone else's return is much more doubtful.[3] One great test of power is to see whether a man who changes sides can make his supporters follow him, and no industrialist seems to have put this to the test. Lord Derby did test the powers of a landlord fairly fully in 1880. About a fortnight after his letter to Lord Sefton explaining that he was going to support the Liberals, he wrote another letter just before polling began which his agent was asked to pass on to his tenants. In it he said that he understood there was some uncertainty whether he had fully joined the Liberals. He therefore wanted it to be clear to all his tenants that he had done so, but that he did not want to influence anybody's

[1] *Daily News*, 24 Mar.; *Deal Mercury*, 6, 13, and 20 Mar. Rigg, op. cit., p. 69. On Brecon, *Hereford Journal*, 10 Apr.; this was a Conservative newspaper and may have underestimated the general anti-Conservative feeling in Welsh seats.

[2] Saunders, op. cit., p. 227; *Manchester Guardian*, 31 Mar.; J. A. Thomas, *The House of Commons 1832–1901* (London, 1939), pp. 14–16.

[3] The statement in John Vincent, *The Formation of the Liberal Party* (London, 1966), p. 97, that 'The notables controlled the town through their ascendancy in party cabals as working politicians, not as employers through the factory' seems generally true. A contrary view is suggested by H. J. Hanham, *Elections and Party Management* (London, 1959), p. 71. Hanham speaks of Ashton being in the pocket of Hugh Mason. Ashton was no more in Mason's pocket than Midlothian was in the Duke of Buccleugh's: Ashton went Conservative in 1874, as Midlothian went Liberal in 1868.

vote. As the Conservatives quickly pointed out, it clearly was an attempt to influence votes, and the suggestion that his tenants might not know that he had changed sides seems most implausible. The power of the united Lancashire landlords was enough to resist the transferred Derby influence in some seats, the Liberal success in South-East Lancashire was to some extent due to the party's revival in Manchester and Salford, and successes in North-East Lancashire and in Derbyshire owed a good deal to the Devonshire interest. This is not to say that Derby's letter had no effect or that the alarm of the Conservatives at the news of his resignation from the government in 1878 had been unjustified. A good deal of his power lay in the Lancashire boroughs, where the landlord's interest was faced with other influences. Lady Derby realized, before the second letter was sent out, that his influence could not be exerted as quickly as she had hoped, and she quoted a Liberal who had said to her, 'Oh my Lady, if only you had been a little sooner in the field'; this man obviously felt that a landlord could change his tenants' views but could not change them overnight.[1]

Apart from this limitation, landlords had considerable electoral power—it may not have differed in kind, but it certainly differed in degree from the power of the industrialists. It was very hard for a man without considerable estates to appear as a serious candidate in a rural county constituency. Landlords possessed the established wealth and position, and the unworried self-assurance, that consolidated their position in the constituencies. In the last resort they also possessed the right to evict their tenants, usually without paying compensation, which meant that the tenant forfeited his investment. This power was used infrequently in England, frequently in Ireland, Scotland, and Wales.[2] Tenants may have been better treated in England because landlord–tenant relations were better, or because English

[1] Derby's letters, *The Times*, 15 and 30 Mar. Speech of Cross, *Daily News*, 2 Apr. Lady Derby to Granville, 28 Mar. and Rathbone to Granville, 9 Apr.: P.R.O. 30–29–27. On Derby's influence see *Dod* and Monypenny and Buckle, op. cit., ii. 1104.

[2] *Daily News*, 7 Apr.; Godley to Granville, 8 Apr.: P.R.O. 30–29–27; Hanham, op. cit., pp. 13–14.

tenants were politically docile; one of the difficulties of assessing an electoral situation in which coercion is a latent factor is the problem of deciding about the motives of the quiet and sober people who do what their superiors want without being threatened. What can be seen is the decline in landlord influence that took place when their economic position *vis-à-vis* their tenants was weakened, but their economic weakness also made them less anxious to be good landlords and this may have caused the fall in their influence.

A landlord normally fought where he had estates. The Conservatives could find suitable candidates without too much difficulty, and the Liberals tried to avoid pitting un-propertied candidates against landlords. They took a great deal of trouble bringing forward landed, and if possible noble, candidates like Lord Lambton and Lord Moreton. People were surprised when the Hon. Robert Spencer stood in South Nottinghamshire, where the Liberal organization was efficient, rather than in North Nottinghamshire where the family estates lay. On the other hand, a reputation as a bad landlord was a handicap; in East Devon the only hope for the Liberal candidate seems to have been the feeling that his opponent kept up rabbits rather too well, and in Here-fordshire Peploe suffered because he was believed to be a stern landlord.[1]

No interest directly opposed the landlord interest in the way that the Church interest and the Chapel interest were aligned against each other in most constituencies. Sermons, for instance, sometimes had a heavy political content. It is hard to tell what sort of clerical intervention was taken for granted and what would cause alarm. The nonconformists may have been a little more active on the Liberal side than the Church of England was on the Conservative side in this election, because of High Church dissatisfaction with the government. The Public Worship Regulation Act had been intended to appeal to the bulk of the Church of England and to gratify popular anti-Catholic feeling. It was a disappointment. So much trouble was caused by the

---

[1] *Morning Post*, 25 Feb.; *The Times*, 9 Mar.; *Exeter and Plymouth Gazette*, 27 Mar.; *Hereford Times*, 27 Mar.; Northcote's speech, *The Times*, 16 Apr.; *Northampton Mercury*, 1 May.

prosecutions of the Reverend Alexander Mackonochie and the Reverend Arthur Tooth for Ritualist practices that the Church cannot have been grateful for the Act and may even have had some sympathy for the opposition to it that Gladstone and Lord Selborne had put up. In the Eastern crisis many Churchmen had supported the cause of the Balkan Christians, and five bishops had served among the conveners of the St. James's Hall conference. It is not necessary to go as far as the pro-Ritualist weekly the *Church Times*, which claimed that the Liberals had won largely because so many Churchmen had supported them, to see that the Conservatives were less able to rely on the Church than they had been in 1874.[1]

Of course Churchmen did come forward. Canon Tristram at Durham said at a political meeting that he was going to speak because the Church was in danger, and then launched into other, more directly partisan topics. On the other side Dr. Dale, a Congregationalist minister, was one of the organizers of the National Liberal Federation and a secretary of the nonconformist lobby for amending the Burial Act. Samuel Morley, who was in some ways the leading nonconformist representative in Parliament, sent a telegram to Northampton in support of Bradlaugh—later on, when the election was over, he said he had been too hasty and regretted it. Spurgeon expressed general support for the Liberals, though when he heard that he was supposed to have told people he would vote for the Devil rather than a Tory, he denied the rumour. Nonconformist chapels were said to be used as committee rooms and as halls for meetings; at the National Union post-mortem on the election it was claimed that Conservatives never took to the pulpit in the way Radicals did, but the effect of this complaint was spoilt by other speakers who regretted that Churchmen had not come forward until it was too late.[2]

---

[1] 'The Beaconsfield Sermon', National Liberal Club pamphlets, vol. 6497; 'Conservative Foreign Policy', an address by the Revd. W. Elwin, Conservative Central Office pamphlets; a sermon reprinted in the *Devon Weekly Times*, 2 Apr., told people to choose carefully, but hinted that the Liberals were the better choice: R. T. Shannon, *Gladstone and the Bulgarian Agitation 1876* (London, 1963), pp. 160–90; *Church Times*, 16 Apr.

[2] *Durham Chronicle*, 26 Mar. and 2 Apr. Dale was an Honorary Secretary, and

Clergymen may have had an illegitimate political influence—that is, an influence which depended on their authority over their flock rather than on political argument—but it was not corrupt. The government influence in dockyard seats was fairly clearly corrupt, although it may have depended on discrimination rather than bribery. The cost of putting pressure on dockworkers by giving contracts on a basis of party loyalty rather than merit was probably very slight, and discriminating among shopkeepers may have cost nothing at all. Political discrimination when shopping was not at all easy in large towns, partly because shops did not depend so much on the custom of single large purchasers and partly because it was impossible to drill so many people. Discrimination in shopping made sense only in constituencies that already inclined so much to one side that there was no real contest, because otherwise the victims of one side could be helped by the other, just as it was a mere freak for an urban landlord to evict a tenant for political reasons. Archdeacon Holbech of Henley-on-Thames dismissed his tailor for making a pro-Liberal speech; presumably it was not too difficult for Liberals to rally round to help the tailor. The people who could apply real pressure were landlords whose evicted tenants would forfeit their improvements and employers who had a monopoly of jobs in a town; the government had something of this sort of power in dockyard towns.[1]

One aspect of the election that conflicted with mid-twentieth-century ideals was plural voting, which was

Schnadhorst the Secretary, of the Central Nonconformist Committee; *English Independent*, 12 Apr. 1877. Morley's telegram was printed as a poster, Nuffield Collection, folio vol. iii, *Northampton Mercury*, 24 Apr. For Spurgeon, *Manchester Guardian*, 26 Mar., and *The Times*, 12 Apr. *Minutes of the 1880 Conference of the National Union.*

[1] Discrimination was recommended in a letter to the *Hereford Journal*, 17 Apr. A letter to the *Spectator*, of 10 Apr., said it was brave of shopkeepers to vote Liberal. A correspondent asked if it was fair for the Chelsea Liberals to boycott Tory public-houses; *Globe*, 23 Mar. The Duchess of Westminster closed her accounts with Liberal tradesmen. Cork to Granville, 5 Apr.: P.R.O. 30–29–27. On the other hand, it was said that shopkeepers put pressure on their customers. *Minutes of the 1880 Conference of the National Union.* For a Greenwich landlord, *Daily News*, 16 Apr. Archdeacon Holbech, *The Times*, 12 Feb. For a different view about the effectiveness of discrimination in shopping, at a slightly earlier period, see J. Vincent, op. cit., pp. 101–4.

particularly prevalent in county seats. A borough voter had to live in, or within seven miles of, the town or city in which he wanted to vote, and anyone wanting to vote on an occupation qualification in a county naturally had to prove residence. A forty-shilling freehold gave an unqualified right to vote (to an adult male). Gladstone had his doubts about this system; in his first Midlothian speech he asked 'Is it not enough that the man who has property in six or ten counties can give a vote in respect of that property . . . in every one of those counties', and he went on to say it was very rare to meet a poor man who had more than one vote and very rare to meet a gentleman who did not have more than one vote. A plural voter had to cast his vote in person—except for the university seats, where there was a postal vote—and this reduced his opportunities slightly. However, as voting was spread over a week or two and candidates were allowed to pay travelling expenses, this was not a very great limitation. County candidates offered railway passes to non-resident voters in the advertisement columns of the newspapers, and sometimes asked for pledges of support despite the law, or paid more than the cost of the ticket, which was also against the law.[1]

None of this was regarded as objectionable until it slipped into faggot-making: creating a nominal property qualification for non-residents. It is as clear as can be that the Duke of Buccleugh created faggot votes to help his eldest son in Midlothian, and it looks as though the family was a little ashamed of it. One of his younger sons wrote an unconvincing letter to the *Daily News* denying that faggots were being created. In the event the creation was not successful; the majority of the owners of newly created freeholds did not qualify for the vote until November 1880. Adam had guessed that something like this might be tried, and had delayed the announcement that Gladstone would stand

[1] Speech of 25 Nov. 1879; *Speeches in Scotland*, i. 15. Johnson, who won an Exeter seat for the Liberals, voted in Middlesex, East Surrey, Mid Surrey, and the Isle of Wight. *Devon Weekly Times*, 23 Apr. Gladstone had votes in Marylebone, Lancashire, Flintshire, the City of London, and Oxford University. *Daily News*, 25 and 26 Mar.; *The Times*, 1 Apr. Electoral law can be followed in *Rogers on Elections*, edition of 1880. Nine advertisements in *The Times*, 5 Apr. *Winchester Observer*, 28 Feb. Debate of 16 Mar., 3 *Hansard*, ccli, col. 1149-50.

accordingly. The new register, with the faggot voters of the second creation, would also have contained an accession of Liberal voters; houses for workmen were being built in the county, just outside the Edinburgh constituency boundary, and the houses were known to be intended for devoted Liberals. Their position would have been a little different from the Duke's faggot voters; the workmen had to live somewhere and would get one vote for their residence wherever it was. On polling-day in Midlothian there were no disturbances, perhaps because few faggot votes had been created early enough. In the neighbouring county of Peebleshire faggot votes had been created in good time, but when the non-residents came to vote, they were stoned and spat upon, so that a chain of policemen had to be formed to escort them to and from the polling station. The *Pall Mall Gazette* complained at this interference with their right to vote.[1]

Bribery was much more widespread than faggot-voting, though people were equally unwilling to confess that they had taken part in it. So far as the evidence goes, one class of constituency was particularly likely to be corrupt: English boroughs with one thousand to eight thousand voters formed a 'corruptible class' and were particularly vulnerable if they had existed before 1832. Boroughs with under a thousand voters were apt to fall into the hands of a single family, and it seems that when the electorate was above eight thousand, candidates were restrained by the great cost of bribing so many people; of course, they may have been restrained from petitioning by the cost, which also increased with the size of the electorate.[2] Despite the steady rise in the number of

---

[1] One hundred and twenty-six voters were added to the lists by faggot-making, another 260 were to follow. *Scotsman*, 12 Feb., 22 and 25 Mar. Letter of Lord Henry Scott, with editorial comments, *Daily News*, 20 Feb.; Adam to Gladstone, 17 Jan. 1879, which contains an assurance that 'we never condescend to faggot-making': Add. MSS. 44095, f. 77; the Tynecastle building prospect, *The Times*, 18 Feb. It was said that Bradlaugh owed his election in 1880 to the enfranchisement of some of his supporters with the help of a co-operative building society, J. M. Robertson, *Life of Bradlaugh* (London, 1894), p. 47. Nuffield Collection, folio vol. iii; *Pall Mall Gazette*, 9 Apr. Other cases of faggot-making mentioned: North Northumberland, Godley to Granville, 8 Apr.: P.R.O. 30–29–27; Huntingdonshire, *Pall Mall Gazette*, 13 Apr.; North-East Lancashire, 'The Reign of Bunkum', *Blackwood's Magazine*, May 1880.

[2] Hanham, op. cit., p. 263, lists sixty-four constituencies. For comments on small but hard-fought seats, Wolverton to Granville, 2 Apr.: P.R.O. 30–29–27;

contests between the Second and the Third Reform Acts, the number of successful petitions remained about the same, which suggests that corruption was not becoming more widespread.

	1868	1874	1880
Contested constituencies	280	299	350
Petitions presented	82	30	42
withdrawn	32	8	14
successful	19	15	17[1]

Of the forty-two petitions launched after the election, twenty-four were in constituencies of the 'corruptible class' and five others were in boroughs of under a thousand voters in which no single family had established control. It may be noted that in constituencies of this type rioting, which may have been a sign of attempts at mob intimidation of voters, took place.[2] The irregularities of elections in these boroughs is not a sign that they were unusually wicked, or even particularly old-fashioned. Some of the irregularities must have been caused by the fact that in a small constituency each vote was especially valuable, and it was worth taking more trouble to obtain it than was the case in a large constituency. In London boroughs the aggregate vote cast was not much larger than the number of registered voters, and as these were two-member constituencies in which 'plumping' for one candidate was uncommon, it appears that about sixty per cent. of the registered electors cast their votes.[3]

Beaconsfield to Lady Bradford, 29 and 31 Mar., Disraeli, *Letters to two Noble Ladies* (London, 1929), ii. 264–5; Rigg, op. cit., pp. 44–46. Family boroughs include Calne (Fitzmaurice), Chichester (Lennox), Hertford (Cecil), Ludlow (Clive), Malton (Fitzwilliam), Marlborough (Bruce), Richmond (Dundas), Tavistock (Russell), Woodstock (Churchill), Wycombe (Smith and Carrington). This excludes county constituencies, or boroughs where a family could expect one seat out of two, as the Peels could at Tamworth. It will be noted how many fewer constituencies were marked in *Dod* than had been the case in previous decades.

[1] 'Bribery and Corruption', *Nineteenth Century*, Nov. 1880.

[2] *Winchester Observer*, 10 Apr.; *East Suffolk Gazette*, 13 Apr.

[3] In the nine double-member boroughs of London,

	1874	1880
Registered	251,833	313,511
Votes cast	225,155	381,496

Some of the increase in votes cast was due to Dilke's Act of 1878 extending voting hours in London to a twelve-hour period as against the normal eight hours.

This would have been a low proportion in a small borough, though it does not follow that the electorates of small boroughs were more interested in politics than those of large boroughs: it was in large boroughs and not in small boroughs that the new organizations began their work. It seems to follow that high turn-out, and irregular practices, were the result of candidates concentrating on winning each individual vote in the small boroughs.

Boroughs which had existed before 1832 were particularly exposed to a danger of corruption. The Great Reform Bill had abolished most of the franchises by which poor men obtained the vote before 1832. Individuals retained their own right to vote but could not pass it on to their descendants unless they had been burgesses or freemen, and by 1880 residence had become necessary for the hereditary burgesses and freemen to qualify. Dod listed 197 seats in which ancient-right franchises still existed:

England Single-member seats	Double-member seats	Scotland Single-member seats	Wales Single-member seats	Ireland Single-member seats	Double-member seats
47	55	1	11	17	5

Resident hereditary burgesses and freemen sometimes made up an economically exposed section of the electorate. Most of the voters, even after 1867, were men with a modest competence, for those who sank in the economic scale usually forfeited their votes. Impoverished freemen and burgesses retained their votes, and they could have argued if no political party would put forward a policy that would help the poor, they might as well make what they could at the election.[1]

There is no sort of agreement on the cost of the election. The returned expenses came to over one and a half million pounds: some illegitimate expenditure probably appeared in the total, because wages paid to messengers, canvassers, flagmen, and so on were probably included. In theory people employed by the parties were struck off the register, but it is clear from the petitions that the judges were unworried

[1] See the rhyme 'Wot's the Use of a Wote—Bill?' in Nuffield Collection, quarto vol.

about this. Money spent for bona-fide organizational purposes was accepted as legitimate, but money spent to give a
bribe under colour of employment (colourable employment)
was not accepted.[1]

As the estimates of total expenditure vary between two
million and three million pounds, it is hard to get any sort of
agreement on the unreturned expenses. It is still harder to
estimate the effect of corruption on the fortunes of the
parties unless one takes the cheerful view that bribes tend to
cancel out. Emanuel, who thought the election had cost
two million pounds and had been twice as expensive as any
previous contest, declared 'It has been shown that . . . the
Tory expenditure rises from 25 to 30 per cent. above that of
the other party'. This statement may have been based on the
returned expenses, which did show a higher level of Conservative spending. For what it is worth on the other side,
Lord Randolph Churchill said the Liberals had bribed much
more heavily than the Conservatives, though he admitted
that Conservative bribery had been quite large enough
to make it impossible for them to expose the Liberals' mal-
practices. He produced no evidence for his statement, and
he may only have wanted to convince the Conservatives
that bribery would not help, because they were not rich
enough.[2]

Because proceedings had to begin with a petition, the
records are not a satisfactory guide to corrupt practices. The
winners would not petition, so bribery which gained voters
but failed to win the seat would not be exposed. Losers would
petition only if they expected to be given the seat or to win
the by-election, because petitioning was expensive even for
the successful side. Rigg thought there would be more
petitions than in 1874 because the Liberals had won both
seats in a large proportion of the two-member boroughs, so
that the Conservatives could bring petitions without fear of a
counter-petition. This helps explain a story about the Ips-
wich election. The Liberals had expected to win, though they

---

[1] *Rogers on Elections*, pp. 359–60.

[2] £2,000,000, *The Times*, 1 Apr.; £3,000,000, Speech of de Ferrieres on 4 June
1883; 3 *Hansard*, vol. 279, col. 1672. L. Emanuel, *Corrupt Practices at Parliamentary Elections* (London, 1881), pp. 15–16. *Minutes of the 1883 Conference of
the National Union.*

calculated there were about a thousand votes for sale in the town. Early in the contest they seemed to be doing well so Cobbold, one of the Conservatives, bought votes at £5 each and, partly to avoid a petition, told these voters to support him and the Radical Collings. As the story was told by the unsuccessful Liberal, it may not be entirely reliable, but there was no petition.[1]

Thirteen Liberals and five Conservatives lost their seats for corrupt practices. This may show that the Liberals gave bribes more often, but because winners never petitioned it may show only that there were more Conservative losers in the boroughs and that Conservative winners were concentrated in the counties, where petitions were rare. The by-elections after Gladstone had formed his government are enough to show that the Liberals had no monopoly of vice. The Conservatives gained seats at Wigtown, Oxford, and Sandwich, and this satisfied them that their defeat at the general election had been caused by local and temporary factors. Petitions were presented in all three places, and produced evidence shocking enough to lead to Royal Commissions in Oxford and Sandwich.

Petitions were very much a matter of tactics. They were withdrawn not because the losers had become convinced of the winners' innocence but because the winners had counter-evidence or were willing to come to a compromise or could weaken the evidence against themselves.[2] As it was in effect only after a petition that a Royal Commission could take place, the evidence of the Commissions must not be taken to cover the whole area in which bribery was practiced, though they are very useful for showing the conditions in a town in

---

[1] The petitions for this election have been studied very closely in Cornelius O'Leary, *The Elimination of Corrupt Practices in Elections, 1868–1910* (London, 1962), pp. 135–56. This book contains a chapter on 1880 which is very useful; the author is concerned with practices that were illegal in the period under consideration; Rigg, op. cit., p. 65; West to Granville, 28 Mar. and 2 Apr.: P.R.O. 30–29–27. The findings of the eight Commissions were summarized in *Parl. Papers*, 1884–5, lxii. 259.

[2] Manœuvres in Leominster and Hereford are described in the Conservative *Hereford Journal*, 17 and 24 Apr., and the Liberal *Hereford Times* for the same dates. The absence of a petition in Dover is striking in the light of Liberal comments on the corruption there. Stanhope to Gladstone, 27 Mar. and 3 Apr.: Add. MSS. 44462, f. 292 and 44463, ff. 42–43. Walker to Granville, 10 Apr. and Sydney to Granville, 14 Apr.: P.R.O. 30–29–27.

which corrupt practices had been proved. In some towns corrupt practices went unproved because blocking petitions were presented, and then withdrawn when it was too late for anyone else to present a genuine petition. The indemnities against criminal proceedings that were given to everyone, however guilty, who confessed were useful for collecting evidence, but in other ways they were a mixed blessing. The result was that nobody was punished, but the electorate as a whole might suffer by losing its parliamentary representation temporarily or permanently.

Treating, or providing free drink, was closely connected with bribery and led, by natural stages, to disorder. It was felt that 1880 was a quieter election than 1874, which had been quieter than pre-Ballot elections.[1] Publicans in 1880 were not pouring out drink to defend their own interests as they had been in 1874. De Ferrieres suggested, when estimating the cost of the election, that most of the money spent on illegitimate expenses ended up in the hands of the publicans, and Rigg also said that very little of this money was kept by the voters.[2] Treating was certainly widespread in some places, but then so was bribery and it is very hard to know what happens to money paid as bribes. In Boston 600 people had been bribed, but even more people had been treated. At Chester 80 people had been bribed, but the bulk of the expenditure had been in the form of excursions and treats given by the sitting members before the election. In the Oxford by-election Hall, the Conservative candidate, was a local brewer and owned seventy public houses in the town; treating was to be expected, though there was also bribery, financed to a considerable extent by the Carlton Club. The Commission advised against allowing a by-election after Hall had been unseated. Sandwich was uncontested at the general election because the Conservatives had no desire to challenge the moderate and popular sitting Members. When Knatchbull-Hugessen was given a peerage just after the election, a Conservative candidate appeared at the by-election. About 2,000 people were entitled to vote, about 1,850 did so, and 1,005 were discovered to have been bribed. It is conceivable that these two Conservative victories

[1] *Standard*, 26 Mar.; *The Times*, 1 and 2 Apr.   [2] Rigg, op. cit., p. 45.

were helped by a feeling that the government had too large a majority, but it is quite clear that what happened at these by-elections was not just a traditional distribution of gifts to known supporters; Commissions had often heard this excuse and as a result they avoided asking people whether their voting intentions had been changed by anything they had received.[1]

Performances like these may have been reduced by the Ballot, though it is true that a good deal remained to be achieved by redistributing the constituencies. When Hartington, Cross, Gladstone, or the tenant farmer candidates reminded voters of the secrecy of the Ballot, it was fairly clear that pressure from the other side was expected. A Conservative agent in Ireland, and the Conservatives at Lynn, hinted that the Ballot was not secret; presumably they had some influence to call upon. The complaints, almost all from Conservatives, that people had broken their promises about voting do suggest that the Ballot was protecting people from pressure that would otherwise have been hard to resist. Of course, some people may have said they would vote Conservative merely to get the canvasser off their doorsteps, but it is most unlikely that this is the whole story.[2]

Corruption and intimidation were the forces that the *Spectator* had in mind when it declared on 24 April, that even if neither party gained any overall advantage by using inducements rather than threats, they might between them debase the quality of the Parliament that emerged, and in particular they might destroy the belief that political leaders could affect the result by the genius with which they put forward rational arguments. However, there were other non-rational devices, which should perhaps be considered more as light relief. Some Liberal candidates had disreputable political pasts: Dilke and Chamberlain had of course been Republicans, and this was pointed out. Firth, who

[1] *Parl. Papers*, 1881, vols. 38, 40, 44, and 45.
[2] The Duke of Cleveland told Granville on 25 Feb. that since the introduction of the Ballot he left his tenants in peace and presumed that they exercised their own judgement: P.R.O. 30–29–27. He later made it clear that he retained his Liberal allegiance, *Manchester Guardian*, 31 Mar. Speeches in *Manchester Guardian*, 27 Mar., *The Times*, 2 Apr.; *Hereford Times*, 20 and 27 Mar.; *Parl. Papers*, 1880, lvii. 575–85 is devoted to refuting Finigan's claim that the Ballot was not secret; on Lynn, *Manchester Guardian*, 24 Mar.

stood with Dilke, was also accused of being a Republican, but later received an apology. Bradlaugh's atheism was notorious; Bryce was also accused of atheism, and demanded an apology. During the Buckinghamshire by-election Lord Stratford suggested to Granville that he ought to find some ardent and irresponsible orator who would remind people that O'Connell had once called Disraeli a descendant of the Impenitent Thief—this was clearly not the sort of thing that a candidate should say himself.[1]

In addition to these pieces of artless vilification there was a little organizational sabotage. The Leicester Conservatives appear to have tried to import a Mr. Simpson, who was being considered as a Liberal candidate in Liverpool where he commanded some Irish and Temperance support, to run him as a third, vote-splitting Liberal, all expenses paid. The Secretary of the Leicester Conservatives wrote a letter of explanation that was not very convincing.[2] One problem of two-member seats was that the voters might, with a little effort, become confused: if a man could be led to vote for one candidate when his party was running two, or to vote for one candidate on his side and one on the other, or for three candidates when he had only two votes, then his party would lose votes. It was possible to go a stage further, to cry 'treason' and say that one candidate had deserted the other man on his side and was only trying to secure his own election, at his partner's expense if need be. Confusion of this sort was likely to be most frequent among the less well educated, and of course most of the pressures discussed in this chapter were of a sort which the rich and powerful could use to affect the decisions of the poor and economically dependent—at a guess, the people who could be misled or subjected to pressure were more often Liberal than Conservative, though this is only a tentative deduction from the much more firmly based premiss that they were poor.[3]

---

[1] *The Times*, 15, 22, and 31 Mar.; 2 Apr. Stratford to Granville, 5 Sept. 1876: P.R.O. 30–29–26.

[2] *Manchester Guardian*, 10 and 19 Mar.

[3] Ibid., 26 Mar., warns voters that a 'plumper' did not have the cumulative force in Parliamentary elections that it had in School Board elections; *Daily News*, 25, 30, and 31 Mar.; *The Times*, 27 Mar.; *Winchester Observer*, 27 Mar.; Saunders, op. cit., pp. 230–1.

The effect of illegitimate pressure must not be exaggerated. It had long been the case that, as Disraeli said in 1848:

You may pass what laws you like, but the ultimate means by which intimidation and corruption will be repressed is by elevating the tone of public feeling, and bringing the influence of public opinion, through the press, to bear upon the conduct of the great body of the nation. It is all folly and nonsense to say that the present age and the present Parliament are distinguished by their corrupt practices. The very reverse is the fact. All Parliaments for the last fifty years have become less and less corrupt. But it is not your laws that have made them so, so much as the increasing action of public opinion.[1]

'The general election of 1880', it has recently been pointed out, 'marked the transition: it was the first general election fought on the national level; it was the last to be disgraced by widespread corrupt practices.'[2] The appearance, and the relative success, of the candidates mentioned at the beginning of this chapter who did not accept the traditional forms of electioneering was a sign of a change in public opinion about the way elections should be conducted. The change was likely to be hastened by every election in which voters thought that they were taking part in something of great moral importance. This ennobling atmosphere, as well as a great and almost final display of the methods of corruption, could be found in the election of 1880.

[1] Debate of 20 June, 3 *Hansard*, xcix. 953.
[2] O'Leary, op. cit., p. 158.

VI

THE RESULT

THE Liberals had won a decisive victory. They held more seats than the Conservatives and Home Rulers put together and while they had almost annihilated the Conservatives in the 'Celtic fringe' they had at the same time gained so many seats in England that they had a comfortable majority in English seats alone.

	England Lib.	Con.	Wales Lib.	Con.	Scotland Lib.	Con.	Ireland Lib.	HR	Con.	Total Lib.	HR	Con.
1874	171	288	19	11	40	20	13	57	33	243	57	352
1880	255	204	28	2	53	7	15	62	26	351	62	239

The change in votes cast was less spectacular, and this must be remembered in considering explanations of the result—the Conservatives were not so completely despised and rejected as the loss of seats would make it appear. The swing to the Liberals cannot be measured in modern terms; one sign that they were attracting more support was that they could put up candidates in seats conceded without a fight in 1874.

	1868	1874	1880
Uncontested constituencies	140	117	66
Unopposed Liberals	113	63	48
Unopposed Conservatives	97	112	58

Of course, most of these seats uncontested in 1874 remained Conservative even in 1880 and the net effect of the increase in contests in 1880, after allowing for constituents contested in 1874 but not in 1880, was to increase the Conservative aggregate by 24,674 more than the Liberal total. So the table of aggregate votes minimizes the success of the Liberals.

	Liberals	%	Conservatives	%	Home Rule[1]
1874	1,263,254	54·2	1,071,325	45·8	83,727
1880	1,801,208	56·1	1,410,650	43·9	94,835

[1] The figures for these tables are taken mainly from McCalmont, *Parliamentary Poll-Book* (London, 1885). Appendix I gives figures for votes, broken down into

Some attempt to give a better comparison can be made by considering only the constituencies which were contested on the same basis in 1880 as in 1874. About 276 seats can be compared in this way, though as they were in the large constituencies they account for well over half the votes cast.

	Liberals	%	Conservatives	%
1874	839,625	55·4	756,817	44·6
1880	1,140,652	58·7	819,865	41·3

The Conservative victory of 1874, with distinctly under half the total votes, was the result of their strength in the counties and the small rural boroughs. They continued to be strong in the small English boroughs as well as the counties.

| | 1874 | | 1880 | |
	Con.	Lib.	Con.	Lib.
Multi-member	86	104	48	142
Single-member	53	39	32	60
30 Smallest	20	10	16	14

In terms of marginal seats 1880 was a close-fought election, and in seventy-two Liberal seats the Conservatives came within 10 per cent. of the winner's vote.

	1868	1874	1880[1]
Liberal	48	49	72
Conservative	48	49	48

There was of course no uniform swing in nineteenth-century elections, but if opinion had been slightly different, and the

smaller categories; it shows that the Home Rule vote was small and not increasing at a significant rate, and the percentages listed here do not include Home Rule. A misprint in W. Saunders, *The New Parliament of 1880* (London, 1880), p. 37, and *Annual Register for 1880*, p. 50, gives too low a figure for contests in 1874. J. P. D. Dunbabin, 'Parliamentary Elections in Great Britain, 1868–1900', *Eng. Hist. Rev.* lxxxi (1966), 82, presents figures from a sample of constituencies that suggest (*a*) a large swing to the Conservatives between the 1868 and the 1874 elections and (*b*) an almost equally large swing back to the Liberals in 1880. This movement of opinion was distinctly larger than anything found here. As the Conservatives polled a majority of the votes cast in 1874 for the seats in his sample, which was not the case in the country as a whole, his sample seems either to have been untypical or (more probably) more volatile than the average constituency. Even so, the Liberals did gain more seats in 1880 than in 1868, which makes one a little uneasy about samples which show they polled better in the earlier election.

[1] H. R. Droop, 'On Methods of Electing Representatives', *Journal of the Statistical Society*, 1881.

Liberals had again lost while polling a majority of the votes cast, there would have been no outburst of indignation. Elections were discussed in language filled with unresolved contrasts: on the one hand, people spoke about the movements of opinion but, on the other hand, they were unworried by the thought of a government holding power although it had polled ten per cent. less of the popular vote than the party in opposition. A shift of 4,054 votes could have cost the Liberals all of the seventy-two marginal seats. Because of the shift in seats, 1880 is regarded as a landslide; in considering the explanations it should be remembered that the election was a near-run thing. (And Gladstone might have added that it would not have been won if he had not been there.)

As the Conservatives were first in the field to offer explanations of the result, it may be useful to begin by looking at their opinions, even if their failure to predict the outcome throws some doubt on their claim to understand the electorate. The explanations offered by the party leaders were in national, not local or regional terms. Beaconsfield made no attempt to minimize the disaster that seemed likely after the first day's results, and attributed it to economic factors in a letter to Salisbury. He called it 'a discomfiture alike vast and without an adequate cause. "Hard Times", as far as I can collect, has been our foe, and certainly the alleged cause of our downfall'. He wrote to Lady Bradford, on the same day, in practically the same words. Salisbury was inclined to agree; Balfour mentioned in addition the lies of Gladstone and the fickleness of the multitude. Northcote also thought that bad times, a hope that change would bring better luck and 'the unscrupulous assertions of our opponents had caused the great defeat'. The Conservative magazines said the Second Reform Act Bill had broken up the steady pattern of British public life. Since 1867 great tidal waves had swept away successive governments. Statesmen could not detect these tides of opinion, and the implication was that they were caused by ingratitude and a hope that a new government would do more for the voters. Accordingly they showed no gratitude to Gladstone for the prosperity of the early seventies and blamed Beaconsfield for the depression that followed.[1]

[1] Beaconsfield to Salisbury, 2 Apr.; Salisbury to Beaconsfield, 7 Apr.; Balfour

The Conservatives consoled themselves by saying that their successes in the City and the Home Counties proved that the solid intelligence of the country was behind them.[1] The Liberal view had for some time been that the jobbers on the Stock Exchange preferred the unstable and sensational policy of the Conservatives because it led to frequent rises and falls in prices, and they hinted that foreign influence was strong in the City. They also mentioned the power of the London press, but did not refer to the weakness of their own organization in the Home Counties or the fact that no Liberal with an established national position was standing in London or the Home Counties. Herbert Gladstone did well for a man who had not previously spoken in public and Dilke was acquiring some sort of position; both of them represented causes that were popular in the London boroughs (in which the Liberals held their ground), but neither of them attracted any upper-class support.[2]

The City, Westminster, and the Home Counties were dominated by people prominent in finance and 'society', and it was generally accepted that these interests would be hostile to the Liberals. A process of change, encouraged by suburbanization and by the death of Lord Palmerston, had begun by 1868, the year in which Lord George Hamilton won Middlesex for the Conservatives.[3] The class dominant in London 'society' had had its privileges and advantages reduced by the Parliament of 1868, and by 1880 it feared a further step towards Radicalism. It found Gladstone dull and Beaconsfield amusing; it found imperialism, in the Bonapartist sense of the sixties and early seventies and in the sense of an exciting foreign policy, provided entertainment and added to Britain's prestige.[4] No doubt this section of the

---

to Salisbury, 7 Apr.: Christ Church papers. Disraeli, *Letters to two Noble Ladies* (London, 1929), ii. 226. Andrew Lang, *Life of Sir Stafford Northcote* (Edinburgh, 1890), ii. 149. 'The Liberal Majority', *Macmillan's Magazine*, May 1880; 'The Tory View of the Election', *Nineteenth Century*, May and June 1880.

[1] Apart from the authorities mentioned in the previous footnote, see the speech of Cross in *The Times*, 3 Apr., and the views of the *Standard*, 3 Apr.

[2] Speeches of Gladstone in *The Times*, 13 and 24 Mar.; Hartington, ibid., 15 Mar.; Forster, ibid., 5 Apr. See *Daily News*, 2 Apr.

[3] Lord George Hamilton, *Parliamentary Reminiscences & Reflections* (London, 1917), p. 11.

[4] R. Koebner, *Imperialism* (London, 1964), especially Chapter 6, 'The Estab-

community would have added that imperialism was in Britain's best interests. So it may have been, but it may have appealed to this section for reasons that meant little to the rest of the country. Regional issues were not easy to find in 1880; foreign policy was more than a regional issue, but perhaps imperialist feeling was a regional sentiment which had an effect in the smarter parts of London and the Home Counties.

It is not necessary to take too seriously Bagehot's remark that '"Ten miles from London", to use the old phrase, there is scarcely any real conception of [Beaconsfield]', but this region did have its distinctive features.[1] For instance, the slender foundation of fact for 'the myth of the Moderate Liberal' was probably that a few Liberals in the clubs, surrounded by Conservatives exulting over a strong foreign policy, did decide that Palmerston would have been happier with Beaconsfield than with Gladstone. Conversions in 'society' had been important before the Second Reform Bill, and may still have been thought important in 1880. When the results were known, the *Daily News* printed an advertisement asking for the missing Conservative working man who had last been seen in the company of someone 'who, having been a Moderate Liberal all his life, was now constrained for the first time to vote for a Conservative government'. The Conservative press had devoted too much time and space to the Moderate Liberals who said that, usually for reasons of foreign policy, they were going to vote Conservative. Too many anonymous letters announcing conversion were printed, and it looks as though some newspapers were so sure of the existence of a large body of Moderate Liberals on the brink of conversion that they decided to manufacture some encouragement for them.[2]

The Conservatives allowed themselves very generous estimates of Moderate Liberal support before the election, but afterwards they seemed to think they had received no help from Liberal converts.[3] They may have been too

lishment of Imperialism as a Slogan', covers the shifting but mainly pejorative uses of the word at the time.

  [1] W. Bagehot, *Historical Essays* (London, 1965), p. 295.

  [2] *Daily News*, 8 Apr. On anonymous letters, see G. C. Thompson, *Public Opinion and Lord Beaconsfield* (London, 1886), ii. 256–9, *Hereford Journal*, 27 Mar., *Pall Mall Gazette*, 1 Apr.   [3] *Globe*, 12 Apr.

gloomy, just as they had been too optimistic previously, because almost any policy gains supporters as well as losing them. This would apply to taxation: under the Conservatives income tax had risen from a level of 2*d*. to 5*d*. in the pound, and the Liberals had argued that the need for constantly rising rates of taxation showed that the government was incompetent. No doubt those who paid 3*d*. in the pound more than in 1874 were annoyed by the rise in the rate. However, in 1874 everybody with an income over £100 had paid; as this exemption level had been raised to £150 in 1876 people with incomes between £100 and £150 were slightly better off.[1] The benefits of Conservative taxation extended to the rich. To judge from the Liberal attack on the 1880 alterations in the Probate Duties, gratitude and self-preservation should have encouraged landlords to go out and work for the Conservatives, and even the depression improved the position of people on fixed incomes because it led to a fall in prices.

The Conservatives liked to claim that their support was more high-minded than this. The belief that reasoned faith in Conservative policy, and Conservative financial policy in particular, had inspired their supporters, while irrational economic discontent and minor local troubles could alone make a man vote Liberal, was expressed by Sir Stafford Northcote on 5 April. He referred scornfully to the fact that many voters in East Devon would be swayed by the candidates' readiness to keep down rabbits as an example of the local issues that affected results, and he suggested that an election decided on such issues did not prove that Britain welcomed Russia's foreign policy. A few weeks later he thought Harcourt's defeat in the Oxford by-election was an important proof of the temporary and local causes of the result of the general election, and ascribed the initial defeat at Oxford to overconfidence.[2]

Local considerations sometimes hurt the Conservatives, though they did not lose East Devon and they won the

---

[1] In 1911 more men had incomes between £100 and £150 than had incomes over £150, Guy Routh, *Occupation and Pay in Great Britain 1906–60* (London, 1965), p. 53.

[2] *The Times*, 6 Apr.; Lang, op. cit. ii. 154.

Oxford by-election by extensive and proved corruption. On the other hand, the Liberals lost ground in Greenwich because more money was spent on the fleet under the Conservatives, and the dockyard workers had benefited accordingly. In Maidstone the Liberals suffered because the local railway interest was against them and the timely gift of a knighthood may also have helped the Conservatives. In Rochester one Liberal candidate would not commit himself to the cause of making vaccination voluntary, but a Conservative was more obliging; he won by 99 votes and the anti-vaccinationists were said to have contributed a hundred to his total. These examples point the irony of Balfour's comment, 'There is always a local reason to be found for every defeat: the singular thing being that the local reasons are all on one side'.[1]

The Conservatives argued that one factor operated against them all over the country. After the Second Reform Bill candidates had to visit their constituencies frequently and make speeches from time to time. As parliamentary duties kept the Conservative members at Westminster, the Liberal candidates could build up their positions and, when it came to speech-making, the newly enfranchised class preferred slashing attack to patient defence, which gave the opposition an advantage. The Conservatives acknowledged that each opposition would enjoy this advantage in turn, and they thought it might explain the swing of the pendulum. In none of their explanations did the Conservatives face the possibility that the election had actually been decided on foreign policy. They asserted that 'our foreign policy had done us no harm in the northern towns. Our defeat was mainly due to the distress and misrepresentation'. They seem to have felt a nostalgia for the summer of 1878 and a desire to be sure that they had been popular. But although the Conservatives declined to stick to their pre-election assertions that foreign policy was the decisive issue, it is necessary to see what sort of effect it had on the electoral position of the government.[2]

[1] *Standard*, 8 Apr.; *Truth*, 8 Apr.; Rigg, *Political Parties, Positions and Prospects*, (London, 1881), p. 65; *Cambridge Express*, 17 Apr.; Balfour to Salisbury, 7 Apr.: Christ Church papers.

[2] *Pall Mall Gazette*, 5 Apr.; 'The Liberal Majority', *Macmillan's Magazine*, May 1880; 'The New Ministry', *Blackwood's*, June 1880; Lang, op. cit. ii. 157.

It probably had a considerable effect, and one that harmed the government. In the diplomacy of the Eastern crisis, the government had begun by saying that it stood for the Tripartite Treaty and the integrity of Turkey, and had ended by producing two secret agreements which looked like attempts to join in the partition of Turkey-in-Europe. The Eastern Question had begun to work in favour of the Liberals long before the original policy of helping Turkey had been seen to be impossible. It had ended the desire for tranquillity in politics which had been the background to Conservative success in 1874. Interest in politics was bound to reawaken, but it reawakened in a way that was particularly helpful for the Liberals. Beaconsfield turned out to have committed himself to the Turks further than was wise; Gladstone was able to make a creditable return to public life despite his explicit departure in 1875. Public sentiment certainly preferred the Balkan Christians to the Turks, and even in a contest between Turks and Russians it was not certain that the Turks would be more popular. Inefficiency, polygamy, and Mohammedanism, to say nothing of a government which defaulted on its debts and was no less autocratic than the Russian, all made the Turk offensive. After the heroic Turkish defence of Plevna in 1877 enthusiasm for the Liberals and for the Balkan peoples did diminish. The government's bold strokes won some approval and Berlin was greeted as a great success. The areas in which the government's foreign policy was popular in 1878, such as London, the Home Counties, and Sheffield were areas in which the government did well in the election.

The spirited foreign policy was likely to lose its attractiveness if it was not successful. The defeats in Zululand and Afghanistan forced voters to consider the prospect of the failure of imperialism. Beaconsfield wrote after the outbreak of fighting in Afghanistan: 'So far as I can judge there is a strong and rising feeling in the country respecting this Afghan business. So long as the country thought they had obtained "Peace with Honor" the conduct of Her Majesty's Government was popular, but if the country finds there is no peace they will be apt to conclude there is no honor.'[1] No

[1] Beaconsfield to Salisbury, 17 Sept. 1878: Christ Church papers.

doubt the Liberals would have preferred people to condemn the government on account of the immorality, rather than the cost or the lack of success, of its policy. But as Gladstone said, 'It is very sad, but so it is that in these guilty wars it is the business of paying which appears to be the most effective means of awakening the conscience.'[1]

One curious feature of the election was the small amount of attention paid to events in Europe after the Congress of Berlin. In this way Beaconsfield's manifesto, with its concern for the place of England in the councils of Europe, was ignored. In terms of European diplomacy the Austro-German treaty of 1879 mattered more than the Congress of Berlin, but while its existence was fairly well understood, no reference was made to it. This may have helped the Conservatives by exaggerating the importance of the Congress, but it showed that the electorate's interest in foreign affairs was limited to things that concerned England very directly; it may be guessed that fellow-feeling for Christians did concern the electorate and that the balance of power at the other end of the Mediterranean did not.

Later historians have been unwilling to commit themselves on the question of the popularity of Conservative foreign policy and have tended to stress factors that most obviously damaged the government: the colonial wars and the slower but perhaps more deadly effect of the decline in trade and depression in agriculture. Ensor agreed that the colonial wars damaged the government and added that with 'economic discontent and the Irish vote both on their side, the Liberals swept the board'. He said that to its foes the defeat of the Beaconsfield system was like a victory over forces of darkness, but did not say whether he thought foreign affairs had any particular effect in encouraging this moral attitude. Trevelyan commented that Gladstone's influence lay in the provinces and that his democratic oratory and the Liberals' electoral organization had a great deal to do with the result; it will be seen how these comments fit in with the way Gladstone handled foreign policy.[2]

[1] Gladstone to H. N. Gladstone, 16 May 1879: F. W. Hirst, *Gladstone as Financier and Economist* (London, 1931), p. 312.

[2] E. Halevy and R. B. McCallum, *Victorian Years* (London, 1951), p. 454; R. C. K. Ensor, *England 1870–1914* (London, 1946), pp. 61–64; G. M. Trevelyan, *British History in the Nineteenth Century* (London, 1922), p. 381.

Historians writing in the 1950s and 1960s have sometimes taken an approach that implies earlier historians saw the election in too modern and too rational a way, attributing more importance to factors that applied all over the country and to logical argument than was realistic.[1] Interest and influence did still matter, though one important result of the election was to weaken their grip. Trevelyan at least, whose father was re-elected in 1880, was in some position to assess the changes that took place in the four decades between the election and the appearance of his history. There were writers in 1880 who tried to discuss the election rather than celebrate a victory or explain away a defeat, and their attitude was much closer to that of the Nuffield College election studies than to the notes on influence and patronage to be found in Dod.[2] Rigg and Droop were concerned with statistical analysis of the results, and their studies make it clear they considered they were dealing with an electorate made up of individuals rather than blocks of subservient or deferential voters.

W. S. Saunders's *The New Parliament of 1880* is a work on an altogether larger scale, though the weight of its argument about the causes of the Liberal victory is almost ruined by a lack of attention to psephological detail. Saunders's argument is that the by-elections held just before the election had shown that the government was popular and that as it then lost the election, it owed its defeat to events that took place between the by-elections and the general election.[3] This argument fails because the by-elections were held in places that gave no useful guide to public opinion. It is a commonplace that the Conservative party was made unduly confident by the by-elections, but it is not so often noticed that the Conservatives did better, in the constituencies where by-elections had taken place, at the general election than they had in the by-elections themselves. The Conservatives won Sheffield and Barnstaple, in both of which they

[1] H. J. Hanham, *Elections and Party Management* (London, 1959), p. 191. It was realized in 1880 that the party label was not enough for victory, and the belief that it relieved the candidate of the need to work was described as 'simple infatuation': 'A Tory View of the Election', *Nineteenth Century*, June 1880.

[2] Rigg, op. cit.; Droop, op. cit.; Saunders, op. cit.

[3] Saunders, op. cit., pp. 191–4.

had lost narrowly in the by-elections, Liverpool was un-contested in the general election, and their initial victory at Southwark owed so much to Liberal disunity that its reversal was not surprising.

Saunders thought that the Water Bill, the Probate Duties in the Budget, and Beaconsfield's ill-judged election address caused the Conservative defeat. It seems quite possible that the Water Bill forced the government to dissolve, and the manifesto certainly harmed the Conservatives in con-stituencies which had a large Irish vote but, as has just been shown, the general movement of opinion did not take place at the time he thought it did. But although Saunders's argument is not in itself very helpful, it shows the terms in which a contemporary expected the struggle to be carried on: the broad outlines of the parties might be laid down by sociological factors, but the margin between success and failure was decidedly political factors.[1]

The political factors did not necessarily act directly on the marginal voters; the great difference between the 1874 and the 1880 voting figures is that while the Conservative total increased slightly, many more Liberals came to vote. An increase in the efficiency of party organization might explain this. The National Liberal Federation was a per-manent legacy from the enthusiasm over the Eastern crisis; however necessary the improvement in party organization, it would have been hard to bring about unless there had been a great issue to launch it. In some cases the loss of an election has been enough to inspire a party reorganization, but the general lack of interest in politics, and the memories of Liberal disunion, were great obstacles to reorganization in 1874.

Some nonconformists had been alienated from the party they usually supported—it could be said that a political event, the passing of the 1870 Education Act, had for some of them overcome the normal social pressures leading them to vote Liberal. The return of the nonconformists was not a matter of social pressures triumphing over political feelings: the Eastern agitation, which began as a non-party matter because its leaders distrusted both parties, developed in a

---

[1] Contrast the views discussed in D. C. Moore, 'The Sociological Premises of the First Reform Act', *Historical Journal*, i, 1966, pp. 39–59.

way that led the militant nonconformists of the Education League back to the Liberal party. In any case they had already seen some of the disadvantages of Conservative government for their cause: it had passed an Endowed Schools Act which they liked even less than the 1870 Act, and it had rejected a Burial Bill which might have ended some of their current grievances. People chose their parties, so far as can be seen, for reasons that were closely connected with the day-to-day course of political events.[1]

The improvement in Liberal organization came at a time when the Conservatives were stagnating, though not collapsing. An unusually large number of candidates had been brought forward by the Conservatives in 1874; in 1880 they had sixteen candidates more. Some of them were brought forward to fight hopeless Scottish boroughs and so divert Liberal attention from the vulnerable counties; this stratagem was not widely approved of, but it was a sign of a fairly active organization. In England there were five more candidates than there had been in 1874, though there were complaints that the quality of candidates was not very high.[2]

Neither side had had a strong constituency organization in 1874. The parsons and the publicans who had given the Conservatives assistance then were in 1880 not so wholeheartedly committed to the struggle. It became clear that the Conservatives had not prepared anything to take their place. The party might have launched something like the Primrose League on a basis of imperialism and Tory Democracy—not that this phrase was used very much in the 1870s. They might also have paid more attention to the National Union which, as an organization primarily for working men, was likely to suffer in a depression. The National Union, as has been shown, was not taken as seriously by party leaders in the same way as the National Liberal Federation.[3]

[1] R. T. Shannon, *Gladstone and the Bulgarian Agitation 1876* (London, 1963) pp. 160–90; 'The Liberal Majority', *Macmillan's Magazine*, May 1880; *Daily News*, 22 Mar.

[2] Candidates in Scotland, *The Times*, 23 and 31 Mar.; Rigg, op. cit., p. 22. Quality of candidates, 'A Tory View of the Election', *Nineteenth Century*, May 1880. Criticism of Central Office, Harold Gorst, *The Fourth Party* (London, 1906), pp. 34–36.

[3] Hartington's suspicion and Granville's uneasiness about the National Liberal Federation have already been noted. In the early eighties the National Union became an important source of strength to Lord Randolph Churchill.

The Federation may have received even more attention than it deserved because the Conservatives spent a lot of time attacking the Birmingham Caucus. Just as the persistent attacks on Gladstone made him even more of a hero to his followers, the attacks on the Federation pushed it into the limelight in a way that was less than fair to the National Reform Union, the Central Liberal Association, and to the London Hundreds, most of which were run on Birmingham lines and accepted Radical principles without being affiliated to the Federation.[1] The increase in the Liberal vote probably owed a good deal to the restoration of party unity as well as to the mechanics of organization. Candidates were selected earlier than usual, and this gave the organization more chance to prevent Liberals standing against each other than it had in 1874.

	1874	1880
Constituencies affected by Liberals standing against each other	22	4
Seats Liberals would have won if all Liberal votes had been cast for one candidate	12	1

The effects of divisions in weakening the organization, as opposed to splitting the vote, is hard to estimate, though the position in Southwark, where the Conservative outpolled both Liberals at the February by-election but was defeated by a united party at the general election, does suggest that it had some importance.[2] There were other organizational advantages about putting candidates into the field early: it reduced the possibility that the sitting Member would be the only candidate the voters had heard of, and the Conservatives admitted they had suffered because Liberals had often been first in the field. Adam was praised after the election because he had placed candidates in all but five English boroughs before the election.[3] Whether it was useful to attack seats left uncontested in 1874 is harder to say. In

---

[1] *Daily News*, 13 Apr. Slagg to Granville, 30 Oct. 1875: M. Ostogorski, *Democracy and Political Parties* (London, 1902), i. 218; S. Gwynn and G. Tuckwell, *Life of Sir Charles Dilke* (London, 1917), i. 233.

[2] Rigg, op. cit., p. 107, estimated that twenty seats were lost because of party disunity.

[3] *Globe*, 13 Mar.; *Minutes of the 1880 Conference of the National Union; Daily News*, 13 Apr.

twenty-four two-member county constituencies which had
returned two unopposed Conservatives that the Liberals
fought in 1880, they gained five seats, and those all came
from constituencies where only one Liberal stood, so that
there was no fear that the Liberals would monopolize the
representation.[1] This relative lack of success suggests that
the decisions taken in 1874 on whether to run candidates or
not were fairly sensible. The argument for running candidates was that it tied down the opponents' resources which
might have been used elsewhere, and in any case running
a large number of candidates showed that morale was high.
The argument against a large number of candidates was that
the party's resources could be concentrated on hopeful
seats.[2]

Party solidarity was stronger than in 1874, certainly on
the Liberal side and possibly on the Conservative as well.
The Berwick result is an interesting illustration:

	1874		1880
Liberal	617	Liberal	687
Conservative	533	Liberal	614
Liberal	418	Conservative	552
Conservative	330	Conservative	457

Clearly the most striking change from 1874 to 1880 was the
increase in the number of votes polled by the second-string
candidates for both parties. The effect was that the representation was no longer divided between the parties. In 1874 the
representation was divided in twenty-seven double-member
constituencies in which both parties put forward two candidates. In 1880 it was divided in only eleven such constituencies. Part of this change was probably caused by an
increasing willingness to regard party affiliation as more
important than the candidates' personal qualities, and part
of it was caused by the restoration of Liberal unity. On a
number of other occasions, notably 1868, the Liberal party
was rallied when its leader proposed a great reform which

[1] See letter in *Northampton Mercury*, 20 Mar.
[2] Spofforth's memorandum, Hanham, op. cit., p. 378, and Herbert Gladstone,
After Thirty Years (London, 1928), p. 160, put a case for contesting as many seats as
possible. On the other hand, Salisbury wrote to Beaconsfield on 7 Apr. 1880 that
the party might have done better if they had concentrated on fewer seats: Christ
Church papers.

aroused enthusiasm without driving away potential supporters. Disestablishment would arouse enthusiasm but split
the party, and extension of the county franchise was widely
rather than fervently supported. The accusation that the
government had been politically immoral in finance and
foreign policy united the wide coalition of interests that made
up the Liberal party, was unlikely to offend any particular
interest, and did not reveal the fact that the party did not
have any agreed legislative policy in mind.

   The suspension of discussion about the leadership assisted
the cause of unity. Hartington and Granville remained in
charge, which reassured moderate Liberals, and the loyalty
and enthusiasm of advanced Liberals was retained by the
possibility of Gladstone's return to the leadership. If he had
returned before the election, the moderate Liberals might
have been upset, and he might himself have had to maintain
a degree of restraint that would have dismayed the Radicals.
As a practical politician he knew that a great moral cause
would not win an election by itself. The Eastern Question
provided an issue that roused the eager and the enthusiastic
to give up their time and their comfort to campaigning.
The great mass of the electorate, including the floating
voters and the people who did not always vote, was likely to
need a more tangible issue. In 1880 the point that was most
likely to influence them was the depression, and the Liberals
hoped to show that the government was to blame.

   The government had increased taxation, had raised expenditure, and had failed to diminish the National Debt. At
the present day the second and the third of these steps might
be thought the correct response to depression; in 1880 all
three were regarded as wicked and, to the extent that they
reduced business confidence, they did in fact make the
depression worse. There was still the problem, for the Liberals, of convincing the electorate that unsound finance was
responsible for their misery; it could not be taken for granted
that the electorate would blame the government, and in any
case the people suffering most acutely did not have votes.
Some candidates did think it was enough to show that
the economy had done well under the Liberals and was
doing badly under the Conservatives. Lord George Hamilton

mentioned one Liberal candidate in Lancashire who asked everybody in the audience who was earning less, or was employed less often, than under the Liberals, to hold up his hand. A large number of people held up their hands, and the meeting was a great success. Quite apart from anything the most powerful orators or the most convincing economists could say, a great many voters chose the Liberal party for the reasons that inspired this meeting.[1]

In North Derbyshire the local newspaper noticed that the depression was gaining the Liberals a great deal of support, and the Liberal candidate for Grantham, when arranging for Gladstone to stop there on his journey to Scotland, wrote that the state of trade was bringing in many supporters. In Salford the Liberal candidate claimed to have the support of all the population who were for cheap food and high wages. All these candidates were successful enough for their statements to be taken seriously.[2]

Liberal speakers who wanted a more rigorous argument contended that the government's foreign policy had disturbed trade, and in this way they linked trade and the Eastern Question. It is most unlikely that this argument was well founded, but a glance at the results by regions does suggest that it was effective. The Yorkshire, Lancashire, and Midland area, which was most damaged by the depression, most responsive to the Eastern agitation and most concerned about export trade, had about a quarter of the seats in Parliament; about half the Liberal gains came from this area, and a good many of the rest came from the 'Celtic fringe'. Partly because of the eventual success of Home Rule, the Irish developments look more important in the long run, but it will be seen that the Liberal gain of seats in Wales

---

[1] Real wages had fallen five per cent. between 1873 and 1879, though in fact a man who had kept his job unchanged was slightly better off in 1879. G. H. Wood, 'Real Wages and the Standard of Comfort', *Journal of the Statistical Society*, 1909, pp. 91–103. Speech of Hamilton, *Daily Telegraph*, 13 May. Bath to Granville, 19 April: P.R.O. 30–29–27. A. L. Bowley, *Wages and Incomes since 1860* (Cambridge, 1937), p. 34, says, 'From 1874 to 1880 prices and wages fell in nearly the same proportion'.

[2] *Hayfield and New Mills Advertiser*, 26 Mar. Roundell to Gladstone, 15 Mar.: Add. MSS. 44462, ff. 194–5. Arnold to Granville, 6 Apr.: P.R.O. 30–29–27. Arnold, in Salford, claimed that he had also been supported by the Irish Catholics and the teetotallers, while the Church and licensing interests had been divided.

was larger than the net gains of the Liberals and their Home Rule allies in Ireland. There was something like an agrarian revolt: old-established families like the Wynns lost their hold on counties they had represented for decades, Englishmen were displaced by Welshmen and opponents of Osbourne Morgan's Burial Bill were swept away by nonconformist feeling. The Liberal success in England was not a rural success; Beaconsfield turned out to be correct in his claim, made before rural results began to come in, that he had dissolved before the farmers had time to organize.[1] Liberals gained a total of twenty-nine county seats, but most of them were in industrial counties like Durham, Lancashire, Northumberland, East Worcestershire, and the West Riding of Yorkshire.

GAINS AND LOSSES BY REGIONS*
(the nine university seats are not included)

Region	Lib.	Con.	Con. gross gain on 1874	Lib. net gain on 1874	Lib. net gain on 1868[2]
London boroughs	14	8	1	1	− 5
Home Counties	8	35	4	− 1	− 13
South	29	30	2	9	− 1
South-west	25	26	5	4	− 4
East Anglia	12	22	1	9	. .
East Midlands	27	20	2	13	7
West Midlands	37	12	. .	13	12
The Marches	24	22	. .	8	3
Yorkshire	31	7	1	10	3
Lancashire	20	12	. .	12	10
Four northern counties	27	7	. .	5	4
Wales	28	2	. .	9	6
Scotland	52	6	. .	12	1
The six counties	5	18	4	− 2	. .
Rest of Ireland	73	5	1	9	12

* See Appendix II for composition of regions, results by counties and division between Liberals and Home Rulers in Ireland.

There was no uniform swing of opinion over the whole country. In the 124 English and Welsh borough constituencies in which the 1874 and 1880 voting figures can be compared, 92 show a significant Liberal improvement and 21 a significant Conservative improvement. If the Conservatives had held their ground in the north, midlands, and 'Celtic fringe' as well as they did in the half of the country

[1] Beaconsfield to Salisbury, 2 Apr.: Christ Church papers. Of the 102 seats in England gained by the Liberals, over 70 were in indisputably urban areas—large market towns like Aylesbury and Bedford are not treated as indisputably urban.

[2] For a fuller version of this table, see Appendix II.

which centred on London, the Liberals would have had a very slender majority. As can be seen from the table, the failure to gain seats in and around London was part of the process by which the Liberals were becoming the party of the provinces. For this table the Home Rule party has been included as a section of the Liberal party, which is an accurate classification for 1868 and 1874 though it may be stretching a point for 1880. The overall change between the 1868 and the 1880 position was not large: 49 seats that had been Liberal in 1868 were Conservative in 1880, and 84 seats that had been Conservative in 1868 were Liberal or Home Rule in 1880. Within these limits the comparison with 1868 strengthens the conclusion that the depression, the export trade, and the Eastern agitation were linked in people's minds, and that it was in the areas where all three factors applied that the Liberals improved most conspicuously over their 1868 showing. The Conservative improvement in and around London may have been helped by imperialist sentiment. Organizational factors help explain the change: the transfer of the Derby influence, the increased stature of Hartington, and the rise of Birmingham Liberalism to the point where it could be exported to other constituencies.

Although the Conservatives lost relatively few rural seats, the farmers clearly were dissatisfied with them. The depression and the bad harvests may have made them more critical of the lack of government assistance after 1874 than they had been previously. The Conservatives had done little, while in office, to support their claim to be the 'farmers' friends'. For decades they had said the malt-tax should be abolished, but they left it untouched. Liberal opposition to the Game Laws was no doubt doctrinaire and P. A. Taylor, the leader of the campaign, who sat for Leicester, may not have known as much about it as his opponents, but when the Commons debated the topic on 2 March 1880 the Conservatives were distinctly embarrassed.[1] The tenant farmers and the Radical opponents of the Game Laws may have aimed at different results, but so far as the election went they could agree in opposing the Conservatives. Questions

[1] F. M. Thompson, 'Standard Politics in the 19th Century', *Transactions of the Royal Historical Society*, 4th ser., 15 (1965), pp. 41–42.

like Land Tenure and Local Government also harmed the government; some Liberals may have supported change more because it would hurt the landlord than because it would help the farmer, but Hartington was unlikely to have been inspired by such feelings when he asked the farmers to give the Liberals a trial.[1] The social influences that made farmers Conservatives were still effective, but political and economic forces were making them wonder how long they could maintain their party allegiance.

It may also have been important that Gladstone's oratory could not be brought to bear on the farmers. To assess Gladstone's effect on the whole election, it is necessary to appreciate what his oratory could do to change people's minds. Gladstone could rouse his followers to intense enthusiasm and passionate belief, and many of the uncommitted were swept away: Liddell, the not unsophisticated Dean of Christ Church, regretted that Gladstone was replacing Granville on some university board, as he never felt happy about Gladstone. A week later, Gladstone had visited Oxford, had made a magnificent oration, and Liddell confessed himself overwhelmed.[2]

An account of Gladstone in action at the time of the election may show the effect that he had. After his death, eighteen years later, the following account of his speech made at Marylebone was published:

'Mr. Chairman and fellow-electors of Marrilbone . . .' Never shall I, an unenthusiastic non-party man, forget those tones. 'Gentlemen, this has been a liquid, an aequous Government. You remember what it came in upon?' 'Beer' we shouted. . . . 'And you see what it is going out upon?' 'Water', we yelled. . . . In next day's newspapers this passage read 'Gentlemen, this has been a liquid Government; it came in on beer and it will go out on water.' Gladstone never said that; it is but a miserable paraphrase of what was said—of what *we* said. All through a speech of long tortuous sentences he endowed us with a faculty of apprehension we did not know we possessed.[3]

[1] Hartington's speech, *The Times*, 3 Apr.

[2] Liddell to Granville, 4 and 10 June 1875: P.R.O. 30–29–25. It is hard to believe that the two letters are by the same man.

[3] Arthur Godley, Lord Kibracken, *Reminiscences* (London, 1931), pp. 109–12, quotes and refers to an article in *Outlook*, by W. L. Watson. The passage is less than fair to *The Times* and the *Daily News* for 13 Mar., both of which mentioned the audiences' responses.

Even his opponents were sometimes carried away. There is a well-known passage that describes his hypnotic domination:

Sir, I can only tell you that, profoundly as I distrusted him, and lightly as on the whole I valued the external qualities of his eloquence, I have never listened to him even for a few minutes without ceasing to marvel at his influence over men. That white-hot face, stern as a Covenanter's yet mobile as a comedian's; those restless, flashing eyes; that wondrous voice, whose richness its northern burr enriched as the tang of the wood brings out the mellowness of a rare old wine; the masterly cadence of his elocution; the vivid energy of his attitudes; the fine animation of his gestures;—sir, when I am assailed through eye and ear by this compacted phalanx of assailants, what wonder that the stormed outposts of the senses should spread the contagion of their own surrender through the main encampment of the mind, and that against my judgment, in contempt of my conscience, nay, in defiance of my very will, I should exclaim, 'This is indeed the voice of truth and wisdom. This man is honest and sagacious beyond his fellows. He must be believed, he must be obeyed!'[1]

Some of his speeches in 1880 appear to have converted opponents as spectacularly, and rather more permanently. After Dalkeith had gone down to defeat, a rumour was heard that some of his trusted friends, who had accepted places on his election committee, had changed their minds and voted for Gladstone. In at least one case this was so, for a member of Dalkeith's committee wrote to Gladstone to find out what he should do after changing his mind. In his reply Gladstone weighed the alternatives carefully, beginning by saying, without any suggestion of irony, that he would prefer to consider the problem as if he were Dalkeith and his questioner had been a member of the Liberal committee. On the whole he recommends the man not to vote, and he tells him clearly that he must not vote against his conscience.[2]

The issue of conscience raised in this way was very important to Gladstone's position. He was trusted and admired by the men of conscience, who thought one should do what was right, and distrusted by the men of honour who thought

---

[1] H. D. Traill, *The New Lucian* (London, 1884), pp. 305–6, quoted in John Morley, *Life of Gladstone* (London, 1908), ii. 248.

[2] Copy, in another hand, of Gladstone to R. B. Marshall, 3 Apr.: Add. MSS. 44463, ff. 34–35. See also Nisbit to Gladstone, 27 Nov. 1879: Add. MSS. 44461, f. 85.

one should keep one's word and not tell people who had given their word that they should change their minds. Conservatives made it clear that they did not think Gladstone an honourable man.[1] Without impugning their Christianity or Gladstone's honour, it could be said that they were gentlemen first and Gladstone was a Christian first. To a man in 'society', Gladstone's long, almost incomprehensible explanations suggested that something not quite straightforward was in his mind; to the men of conscience, nonconformists and Anglicans alike, his speeches were the outward sign of a supremely honest man wrestling with his conscience. If the election was fought on these lines, the men of honour would certainly be outnumbered.

The men of conscience would have been uneasy about the party of the men of honour even if Gladstone had been left out of account. The 'eight scandalous jobs', in which it was claimed that people had gained civil service promotion by favouritism, seemed to endanger the prospects that had been opened up when the Liberals extended the examination system and almost eliminated patronage outside the Diplomatic Service.[2] The cry of jobbery was bound to attract support and it also lent weight to complaints that government policy had been conducted in an immoral manner. It has been mentioned that six occasions in the first half of 1878 were picked out for attention; the government's conduct was denounced as 'surprising' and the Liberals argued that policy should be conducted openly and explained openly.[3] Beaconsfield's manifesto was so vague that it seemed to be

---

[1] Disraeli made it clear to Ponsonby that he considered Gladstone had not discussed parliamentary business with the leader of the opposition as between men of the world. Ponsonby to Granville, 4 Feb. 1875: P.R.O. 30–29–25. The Marylebone Conservatives felt uneasy about giving Gladstone a 'pair' for his vote there; they thought he would hurry to London and vote despite the 'pair', *The Times*, 30 Mar.

[2] Speeches condemning the 'eight scandalous jobs', *Daily News*, 17 Mar., *Devon Weekly Times*, 2 Apr. Dasent to Granville, 22 Aug. 1876; on Beaconsfield's detestation of open competition: P.R.O. 30–29–26. After the election Beaconsfield had to be prevented by the Cabinet from appointing Lord Henry Lennox, who had had to retire from the government in 1876 over a transaction in shares, Chief Civil Service Commissioner. W. F. Monypenny and G. E. Buckle, *Life of Disraeli* (London, 1920), vi. 532.

[3] Gladstone's speech of 26 Nov. 1879, *Speeches in Scotland*, i. 18. Speeches of Hartington, *Manchester Guardian*, 30 Mar., 2 and 5 Apr.

asking for a very free hand in foreign policy, and on their side some Conservatives argued that the Liberals were so unpatriotic that they could not be trusted with power.

This argument made the trustworthiness of the parties into an important question. Nobody imagined that Conservatives like Northcote, Cross, and Smith would do anything disturbing, but Beaconsfield, aloof, lonely and silent, was the man whose policy was on trial and it was his character that had to be defended. His character was probably less complex, and his course of action no less consistent than that of Gladstone, but his delight in the sudden and the spectacular, and his readiness to act the part of the Asian Mystery, harmed his party. There were suggestions, perhaps particularly vocal just after the election, that he did not always advise the Queen properly. During the election attacks were concentrated on him, which was tactically wise because it did seem possible that he was unsound and even unscrupulous.[1] 'Sober-minded men don't believe in novel-writing Premiers', and the novels, apart from some flashes of insight, a prophecy or two like the recommendation to occupy Cyprus and a taste for autocracy, were not sedate enough to reassure the electorate.[2] Beaconsfield's extreme coolness and Gladstone's extreme warmth, combined with the fact that they represented polar opposites in their approach to foreign policy, meant that neither of them was trusted by the whole country. Gladstone was the more distrusted in Parliament, Beaconsfield the more distrusted by the electorate.

Even Gladstone's opponents recognized his greatness as a finance minister. This may have made people think he would bring back prosperity with him, and that he might serve as Chancellor of the Exchequer and not as Prime Minister.[3] In other realms of political life he aroused a good deal of hostility. It was true that, as he said, the Liberal party

---

[1] 'The Asian Mystery' was not a compliment. Speech of Beresford-Hope, 12 Apr. 1867; 3 Hansard, clxviii, 1608; Lloyd's Weekly Newspaper, 25 Apr. Watkin Williams called him a despot in posse, The Times, 30 Mar.

[2] W. Ford to W. H. Smith, H. E. Maxwell, Life of W. H. Smith (Edinburgh, 1893), ii. 28. See also Monypenny and Buckle, op. cit. v. 169–70.

[3] 'Mr. Gladstone By a Conservative', Contemporary Review, Nov. 1879; Whitehall Review, 10 Apr.

could not reckon on the wealth of the nation, nor on the rank of the nation, nor on the influence which rank and wealth usually bring, although he admitted that a small part of the influential classes was on the Liberal side. He was over-stating his case when he said that in the 'narrow and sectional interests' there was no friendship and tolerance for the Liberal party, but it was true that there was probably very little friendship and tolerance for him.[1] His statement that the legislature could justifiably buy out landed proprietors, if it was in the public interest, probably upset some people. It showed that he was more willing to be venturesome for the sake of social welfare than is sometimes realized, and it indicated one direction his Irish policy was to take. He was attacked as the worst kind of demagogue, stirring up un-patriotic bitterness at a time of life when he would have done better to stay in retirement—the Liberal attacks on Beaconsfield may have been as violent in conception but were less personal in tone.[2]

The Conservatives' objections to the fierceness of Glad-stone's attacks sometimes revealed a nostalgia for some golden age, probably during the premiership of Lord Palmerston, when politics had been carried on with gentle-manly good feeling and lack of interest.[3] Politics had been hard-fought in earlier decades, and in any case the Con-servatives had at least as much responsibility as the Liberals for the Second Reform Bill and the changed conditions of politics. However, the Conservatives were right to think of Gladstone as a sort of lay-preacher. There was a strong appeal to religious and moral attitudes in the speeches of the Liberals although specifically religious questions were much less important than in 1868 and 1874. Successful speeches were likely to have some elements of the sermon, if they were to suit the taste of a sermon-listening public, and this was all the more likely because several politicians were men of deep religious conviction.[4] Gladstone effectively presented

[1] Speech of 4 Apr., *Speeches in Scotland*, ii. 91.

[2] Speech of 27 Nov. 1879, *Speeches in Scotland*, i. 79. Speech of Dalkeith, *The Scotsman*, 24 Mar. Gladstone called the acquisition of Cyprus an 'insane convention'. Beaconsfield said that only a 'sophistical rhetorician' would have described it in that way, Herbert Gladstone, op. cit., p. 51.   [3] *Globe*, 12 Mar.

[4] The first Midlothian speech (25 Nov. 1879) provides examples: 'let every one

himself as the leader of a crusade for righteousness rather than a politician looking for expedients, and equally clearly regarded his opponents as the incarnation of evil. The Liberals in 1880 might have operated by trying to put together a coalition of interest groups which considered themselves injured by the government in the way that the drink trade and the Church had felt ill treated in 1874. However, the scope of government activity was not wide enough for a party to be able to make generous promises. Until 1867 the vote had been given only to classes so well off that it was hard to think of redistributing money in their favour, and the classes enfranchised in 1867 had not realized that in their position they might gain by state action. They appear to have believed that the only good reason for political action was the prospect of increasing the nation's prestige, or of helping the cause of religion and morality.

Gladstone had a far greater power than any other British statesman has possessed for bringing home to his listeners the moral aspects of a political problem, and this power was revealed at its most intense between 1876 and 1880. He had very strong support within his party; at meetings, his name was the name to be cheered, and the concentration on Gladstone increased the concentration on foreign policy.[1] Some Liberals pointed to Hartington to show that they had a respectable leader, but the effect of attacks on Gladstone was to make him appear the real leader and to some extent the discussion of foreign policy was a disguised way of asking whether people wanted Gladstone. The Midlothian campaign had the same effect of keeping him in the public eye, and this was particularly true of the first visit which took place when there was no other news to compete with. His speeches had time to sink into people's minds, and were put into pamphlet form so that loyal Liberals could study his arguments and reproduce them at need. The second Midlothian speeches could not be circulated in the same way

of us resolve in his inner conscience, before God and before man' and '[Conservative policy is] an appeal to pride and passion'. *Speeches in Scotland*, i. 18 and 30.

[1] *Truth*, 4 Mar.; *Surrey Comet*, 6 Mar.; when Gladstone placed Hartington and Granville before himself, the Marylebone crowd shouted 'No.' *Morning Post*, 13 Mar.; the *Spectator*, 20 Mar., said the enthusiasm for Gladstone could be compared with 1868 (when he was the official leader).

and active politicians may have been too busy to study them as closely. The enthusiasts in the party organization, who were the people outside Midlothian itself most likely to be inspired by the campaign, did know after November 1879 that Gladstone was remaining in public life although the Eastern Question was closed, and they would remember in April what he had said five or six months earlier. Presumably reasoning of this sort lay behind a friend's comment to Gladstone, 'Your Scotch campaign in November won the fight'.[1]

The victory was won by a narrow enough margin in votes to mean that a whole variety of factors could be considered decisive in the sense that they put potential voters into the mood to vote Liberal or that they provided the additional energy needed by the party organization if it was to make use of this mood in the electorate. The great victory was not won merely by enunciating moral principles and championing people rightly struggling to be free, and it could be argued that his failure to do anything about the social conditions which made the electorate ready to turn to the Liberals showed that Gladstone had misread the lessons of the election. On the other hand, in the years before the election it was the Conservatives who neglected their opportunities. Beaconsfield did nothing to turn the enthusiasm of 1878, or such gratitude for social reform as there may have been, into anything durable in the form of party organization. The Liberals, by creating the National Liberal Federation, did do something to make permanent the party energy provided by the Eastern Question.

The fate of the great Liberal majority, which eventually fell apart over Ireland, may be a warning against neglecting economic issues. People probably thought about such issues much less than they do in present-day elections, simply because neither party was really expected to do very much about them. In 1880 neither party was particularly worried about the relatively high unemployment, largely because nobody thought the politicians could do much about it. On the wider issue of the state of trade, many people felt all

---

[1] Oakeley to Gladstone, 10 Apr.: Add. MSS. 44463, ff. 90–91. See *Daily News*, 20 Apr.

would be well if the Liberals could form a goverment, balance
the Budget, and restore merchants' confidence by not threatening to go to war. This programme was not really likely to
have any effect on the depression, and it was the last time
that an election could have been fought on so narrow a view
of economic circumstances.

This is not the aspect of the campaign that makes the
election memorable, though it may help to explain its place
in the development of the British party political struggle.
In the wider history of democracy, in which this election
holds a conspicuous place, the important aspect was concern with foreign policy, and in particular with Gladstone's handling of it. The parliamentary system did not
offer much chance for anybody to benefit economically from
political change, and so it was unlikely that anyone would
sacrifice their time and their money to political activity
except from a sense of moral obligation. Rich men would
respond to the aristocratic tradition that they should do
something for their country with their time and money, and
before the Second Reform Bill this had been enough to keep
the parties going. After a few decades the scope of government activity would become so great that many people felt
there might be some economic advantage in political activity.
In the intervening period men had to be roused to come
forward and fight for a great moral cause. This was the
period of triumphant platform oratory, of great leaders
addressing massed audiences, and proclaiming crusades
for noble ideals.[1]

It was a situation for which Gladstone's gifts were suited
perfectly. He went forward as the champion of the ideals
of Christianity, of freedom, and of justice that were common
to all. Possibly it would have been more statesmanlike
to think in terms of Britain's safety and prestige, though
there is no sign that thinking in these terms led to a policy
which promoted these ends. In any case safety and prestige
were not very compelling ideals in a nation that could not
really believe that Britain's safety was menaced. In the
secure world of the late nineteenth century the great moral

---

[1] Herbert Gladstone, op. cit., p. 161, has some comments on the importance of
party enthusiasm.

absolutes to which Gladstone appealed were bound to weigh heavy on men's minds.

They provided a motive force for the long process of Liberal reorganization, and they lent zeal to the men who had to do the work of getting voters to the polling-booths. Gladstone's speeches gave a moral dignity to a struggle against a policy which claimed to be based on a sensible, realistic approach, and they made the whole struggle seem more important.[1] On the face of it there was no very great difference of policy between the two parties. To make plain the difference of attitude that underlay the slight difference of policy was the object of a good deal of Gladstone's oratory, for this brought out the fact that the Liberals stood for great principles and for progress, and the Conservatives stood for established interests and traditions. Gladstone's strength lay in moral rather than political analysis, so he did not present his arguments in simple political terms, but the logic of his morality was enough to show his audiences the practical advantages that might result from a Liberal victory.

The question of practical advantage was not all-important, for Gladstone managed, much more than anyone else, to make the British electorate see problems in these moral terms. A liking for the commonsense approach, or a surge of national and patriotic feeling, have often reinforced the feeling that the time has come for a change, or that the government is responsible for economic adversity. Occasionally there has been a feeling that social justice has been denied to some people; 1880 can confidently be put forward as the only occasion when a very great impression has been made by a leader whose theme has been the condemnation of one moral attitude, and the enunciation of another. There has been no other British statesman so ready to appeal to moral sentiment, or so able to arouse it in his audiences; this election was the great triumph of the principle that the government should act no less morally than a free and unselfish individual, which was the guiding motive in the political life of Mr. Gladstone.

[1] This is why he was so eager to show that the Eastern Question was the great issue from which all the rest followed. Speech of 25 Nov. 1879, *Speeches in Scotland*, i. 20.

APPENDIX I
ANALYSIS OF VOTES CAST
ENGLAND AND WALES: BOROUGHS

	1874 Liberal		1874 Conservative	1880 Liberal		1880 Conservative
Contested: results comparable from one election to the other						
Votes cast	558,045		472,948	758,883		525,772
Constituencies	124		124	124		124
Seats	183		183	183		183
Candidates	190		171	182		170
Contested: results not comparable: no. of candidates differs from one election to the other						
Votes cast	230,870	66,366[1]	103,618	282,422	9,327[1]	153,598
Constituencies	35	5	30	35	4	31
Seats	59	7	52	59	4	55
Candidates	71	13	46	62	8	45
Seats left uncontested at one election or the other						
Votes cast	57,535	6,276[1]	48,681	90,538		49,375
Constituencies	12	2	10	20		20
Seats	15	2	13	24		24
Candidates	18	2	12	24		23

ENGLAND AND WALES: COUNTIES

	1874 Liberal	1874 Conservative	1880 Liberal	1880 Conservative
Contested: results comparable from one election to the other				
Votes cast	159,972	196,297	215,512	208,814
Constituencies	28	28	28	28
Seats	50	50	50	50
Candidates	42	47	41	47
Contested: results not comparable: no. of candidates differs from one election to the other				
Votes cast	33,860	60,844	36,264	66,221
Constituencies	7	7	7	7
Seats	15	15	15	15
Candidates	11	14	9	14
Seats left uncontested at one election or the other				
Votes cast	27,416	36,820	165,923	229,894
Constituencies	6	6	33	33
Seats	13	13	64	64
Candidates	9	10	49	60

[1] See p. 162 n.

SCOTLAND

	1874		1880	
	Liberal	*Conservative*	*Liberal*	*Conservative*
Contested: results comparable from one election to the other				
Votes cast	108,351	60,141	152,369	55,996
Constituencies	25	25	25	25
Seats	28	28	28	28
Candidates	31	26	28	27
Contested: results not comparable: no. of candidates differs from one election to the other				
Votes cast	18,985 4,079[1]	7,168	20,622	6,998
Constituencies	2 1	1	2	2
Seats	3 1	2	3	3
Candidates	5 2	2	4	2
Seats left uncontested at one election or the other				
Votes cast	12,251 3,600[1]	4,439	27,390 2,150[1]	16,061
Constituencies	5 2	3	17 1	16
Seats	5 2	3	17 1	16
Candidates	7 4	3	18 2	16

IRELAND

	1874			1880		
	Liberal	*Home Rule*	*Conserva-tive*	*Liberal*	*Home Rule*	*Conser-vative*
Contested: results comparable from one election to the other						
Votes cast	13,257	6,631	27,431	13,888	7,472	29,283
Constituencies	12	7	15	12	7	15
Seats	15	9	20	15	9	20
Candidates	12	9	18	12	10	18
Contested: results not comparable: no. of candidates differs from one election to the other						
Votes cast	42,846 482[1]	52,015 4,028[1]	54,541	39,807	60,907 7,382[1]	69,605
Constituencies	25 1	22 1	18	16	21 3	23
Seats	44 1	38 2	29	25	36 6	40
Candidates	38 2	35 3	25	21	40 9	31
Seats left uncontested at one election or the other						
Votes cast	4,425	25,081	351	1,032	26,456 16,728[1]	2,901
Constituencies	6	5	2	2	7 3	4
Seats	10	9	3	3	13 5	6
Candidates	7	11	2	2	16 8	5

[1] The contests recorded in this column were between competing members of the same party. The sub-totals are included in the column immediately to the left.

APPENDIX II

ANALYSIS OF SEATS BY COUNTIES

Region	Liberal	Liberal net gain on 1874	Conservative
London	14	1	8
Home Counties			
Kent	5	−2	14
Middlesex			2
Surrey			7
Sussex	3	1	12
South			
Berkshire	5	1	3
Buckinghamshire	5	2	3
Hampshire	6	4	8
Hertfordshire	1		3
Isle of Wight	2	1	
Oxfordshire	4		3
Wiltshire	6	1	10
South-west			
Cornwall	10	2	3
Devonshire	7	1	10
Dorset	4		6
Somerset	4	1	7
East Anglia			
Cambridgeshire	3	2	2
Essex	3	3	7
Norfolk	4	2	6
Suffolk	2	2	7
East Midlands			
Bedfordshire	4	2	
Huntingdonshire	1	1	2
Leicestershire	3	1	3
Lincolnshire	8	4	6
Northamptonshire	5	2	3
Nottinghamshire	6	3	4
Rutland			2
West Midlands			
Derbyshire	7	2	1
Staffordshire	12	5	5
Warwickshire	10	2	4
Worcestershire	8	4	2

Region	Liberal	Liberal net gain on 1874	Conservative
The Marches			
Cheshire	7	2	7
Gloucestershire	9	4	4
Herefordshire	4	2	2
Monmouthshire	1	1	2
Shropshire	3	—1	7
Yorkshire	31	10	7
Lancashire	20	12	12
4 Northern Counties			
Cumberland	5	1	3
Durham	13	1	
Northumberland	8	3	2
Westmorland	1		2
Wales			
Anglesey	2		
Breconshire	2	2	
Cardiganshire	2	1	1
Carmarthenshire	2	2	
Carnarvonshire	2	1	1
Denbighshire	2		
Flintshire	2		
Glamorgan	6		
Merioneth	1		
Montgomeryshire	2	1	
Pembrokeshire	3	1	
Radnorshire	2	1	
Scotland			
Aberdeenshire	3		
Argyll	1		
Ayrshire	2	1	2
Banffshire	1		
Berwickshire	1	1	
Bute	1	1	
Caithness	2		
Clackmannan and Kinross	1		
Dunbartonshire			1
Dumfriesshire	2	1	
Elgin and Nairn	2		
Fifeshire	3		
Forfarshire	4		
Haddingtonshire	1		1
Inverness-shire	1		1
Kincardine	1		
Kirkcudbright	1		

Region	Liberal	Liberal net gain on 1874	Conservative
Lanarkshire	5	2	
Linlithgow	1		
Midlothian	4	1	
Orkney	1		
Perthshire	2	1	
Renfrewshire	3		
Ross and Cromarty	1		
Roxburghshire	2	1	
Selkirk	1	1	
Stirlingshire	3	1	
Sutherland	1		
Wigtownshire	1	1	1
Ulster			
Antrim		−1	6
Armagh	1	1	2
Down		−2	4
Fermanagh			3
Londonderry	2	−1	2
Tyrone	2	1	1

Region	Liberal	Home Rule	Net Liberal and HR gain on 1874	Conservative	Comment
Rest of Ireland					
Carlow		3	2		
Cavan		2			
Clare		3			Lib. loss
Cork	1	6	— 1	1	Lib. loss to Cons.
Donegal	2		2		
Dublin	1	1	1	2	Lib. gain from Cons.
Galway		4			Lib. loss
Kerry		3			Lib. loss
Kildare		2			Lib. loss
Kilkenny		3			
King's Co.		2			
Leitrim		1		1	
Limerick		4			
Longford		2			
Louth	2	2			Lib. gain
Mayo		2			
Meath		2			
Monaghan	2		2		
Queen's Co.		2		1	
Roscommon		2			
Sligo		2	1		
Tipperary		3			
Waterford		5	1		Lib. loss
Westmeath	1	2			
Wexford	1	3			Lib. gain
Wicklow		2	1		

SELECT BIBLIOGRAPHY

The story of a general election, which is a very diffuse set of events, has to be told by picking through a large number of different sorts of material, and it is sometimes hard to decide how many references are needed to establish a point. Simple events can sometimes be supported by a single authority, but in attempting to define a party's policy, or to show that an issue was prominent, a little repetition is necessary. References of this sort are made to newspaper editorials and reports and to political pamphlets.

MSS. MATERIAL

Gladstone Papers, in the British Museum.
Granville Papers, in the Public Record Office.
  (The correspondence between the two statesmen can be followed in *The Political Correspondence of Mr Gladstone and Lord Granville* (edited A. Ramm), London, 1952, and London, 1962.)
Salisbury Papers, in Christ Church Library.
Minutes of the Conferences of the National Union of Conservative Associations, in Abbey House, Westminster.

PARLIAMENTARY PAPERS, from the State Paper Room of the British Museum. The most useful volumes are 1880, lvii. 1, Return of Expenses and 53, Registered Voters; 1881, xxxviii–xlv, Reports of the Commissions on corrupt boroughs; 1883, liv. 369, Qualifications by which registered voters hold the franchise.

COLLECTIONS OF PAMPHLETS in the Bodleian Library, the British Museum, the Conservative Central Office, Liberal Party head-quarters (including information about the National Liberal Federation), the National Liberal Club, and Nuffield College (which has, as well as pamphlets, a much larger number of posters than I have found elsewhere).

NEWSPAPERS

London: *Daily News*; *Daily Telegraph*; *Globe*; *Lloyd's Weekly News*; *Morning Post*; *Pall Mall Gazette*; *Standard*; *The Times*.
Provincial: *Cambridge Express*; *Deal Mercury*; *Devon Weekly Times*; *Durham Chronicle*; *East Suffolk Gazette*; *Exeter and Plymouth Gazette*; *Hereford Mercury*; *Hereford Times*; *Manchester Guardian*; *New Mills and Hayfield Advertiser* (indexed at Colindale under Chapel-en-le-Frith); *The Scotsman*; *West Kent Courier*; *Winchester Observer*.

Trade: *Mark Lane Express*; *Railway Service Gazette*.
Between them these newspapers give election addresses for about 200 backbenchers.

MAGAZINES

Weekly: *The Economist*; *Punch*; *Saturday Review*; *Spectator*; *Truth*; *Vanity Fair*; *Whitehall Review*; *The World*.

Less frequent (and, on the whole, more respectable): *Blackwoods*; *Contemporary Review*; *Edinburgh Review*; *Fortnightly Review*; *Macmillan's Magazine*; *Nineteenth Century*; *Quarterly Review*.

WORKS OF REFERENCE

The Annual Register.
Dictionary of National Biography.
Dod's *Parliamentary Companion.*
Droop, H. R., 'On Methods of Electing Representatives', *Journal of the Statistical Society*, 1881.
Hansard, *Parliamentary Debates*, 3rd series.
McCalmont, F. H., *The Parliamentary Poll Book*, 1832–1906. London, 1906.
Rogers, F. N., *The Law and Practice of Elections and Registrations*. London, 1880 (13th edition, ed. Carter).
Statutes of the Realm

BOOKS BY CONTEMPORARIES

Cavendish, Lady Frederick, *Diary* (ed. Bailey), 2 vols. London, 1927.
Disraeli, Benjamin, *The Letters of Disraeli to Lady Bradford and Lady Chesterfield* (ed. Zetland), 2 vols. London, 1929.
Emanuel, Lewis, *Corrupt Practices at Parliamentary Elections*. London, 1881.
Gladstone, Henry, Chapter of reminiscences in F. W. Hirst, *Gladstone as Financier and Economist*. London, 1931.
Gladstone, Herbert, *After Thirty Years*. London, 1928.
Godley, Arthur (Lord Kilbracken), *Reminiscences*. London, 1931.
Hamilton, Lord George, *Parliamentary Reminiscences and Reflections, 1868–1885*. London, 1917.
Lucy, Henry, *A Diary of two Parliaments*, vol. i (*The Disraeli Parliament, 1874–1880*). London, 1885.
Reid, T. Wemyss, *Memoirs, 1842–1885* (ed. S. Reid). London, 1905.
Rigg, T. Galloway, *Political Parties: Their Present Position and Prospects*. London, 1881.
Russell, G. W. E., *Portraits of the Seventies*. London, 1916.
Saunders, W., *The New Parliament of 1880*. London, 1880.

BIOGRAPHIES

Fitzmaurice, Lord Edmond. *Life of the Second Earl of Granville.* 2 vols. London, 1905.

Gardiner, A. G., *Life of Sir William Harcourt.* 2 vols. London, 1923.

Garvin, J. L., *Life of Joseph Chamberlain*, vol. i. London, 1932.

Gwynn, S., and Tuckwell, G., *Life of Sir Charles Dilke*, 2 vols. London, 1917.

Holland, Bernard, *Life of the Eighth Duke of Devonshire*, 2 vols. London, 1911.

Lang, Andrew, *Life of Sir Stafford Northcote*, 2 vols. Edinburgh, 1911.

Monypenny, W. F., and Buckle, G. E., *Life of Benjamin Disraeli*, 2 vols. London, 1929.

Morley, John, *Life of Gladstone*, 2 vols. London, 1908.

Pearson, Hesketh, *Labby.* London, 1936.

Reid, T. Wemyss, *Life of Forster.* London, 1889.

Robertson, J. M., *Bradlaugh.* London, 1920.

Stead, W. T., *The M.P. for Russia, Reminiscences and Correspondence of Olga Novikoff*, 2 vols. London, 1909.

Trevelyan, G. M., *Life of John Bright.* London, 1913.

OTHER BOOKS

Blake, R., *Disraeli.* London, 1966.

Ensor, R. C. K., *England, 1870–1914.* Oxford, 1946.

Gash, N., *Politics in the Age of Peel.* London, 1953.

Gorst, H. E., *The Fourth Party.* London, 1906.

Gwyn, W. B., *Democracy and the Cost of Politics in Britain.* London, 1962.

Hanham, H. J., *Elections and Party Management.* London, 1959.

The History of The Times, vol. ii. London, 1939.

Howard, C. H. D., *Introduction* to '*A Political Memoir*' by *Joseph Chamberlain.* London, 1953.

Humphrey, A. W., *A History of Labour Representation.* London, 1912.

James, R. R., *Rosebery.* London, 1963.

Jephson, H., *The Platform.* 2 vols. London, 1892.

Medlicott, W. N., *The Congress of Berlin and After.* London, 1938.

O'Brien, C. C., *Parnell and His Party.* Oxford, 1957.

O'Leary, C., *The Elimination of Corrupt Practices in British Elections, 1868–1911.* Oxford, 1962.

Ostrogorski, M., *Democracy and the Organisation of Political Parties*, vol. i (trans. Clarke). London, 1902.

Seton-Watson, R. W., *Disraeli, Gladstone and the Eastern Question.* London, 1935.

Seymour, C. S., *Electoral Reform in England and Wales, 1832–1885*. New Haven, 1915.

Shannon, R. T., *Gladstone and the Bulgarian Agitation, 1876*. London, 1963.

Thomas, J. A., *The House of Commons, 1832–1901*. Cardiff, 1939.

Thompson, G. C., *Public Opinion and Lord Beaconsfield, 1875–1880*, 2 vols. London, 1886.

Vincent, J., *The Formation of the Liberal Party*. London, 1966.

Watson, R. S., *The National Liberal Federation*. London, 1907.

ARTICLES IN JOURNALS

Beales, H. L., '"The Great Depression" in Industry and Trade', *Economic History Review*, v (1934).

Crapster, B. L., 'Scotland and the Conservative Party in 1876', *Journal of Modern History*, xxix (1957).

Dunbabin, J. P. D., 'Parliamentary Elections in Great Britain, 1868–1900', *English Historical Review*, lxxxi (1966).

Herrick, F. H., 'The Origins of the National Liberal Federation', *J. Mod. Hist.*, xvii (1945).

Howard, C. H. D., 'The Parnell Manifesto of 21 November 1885 and the Schools' Question', *E.H.R.*, lxii (1947).

Kelley, R., 'Midlothian: a Study in Ideas and Politics', *Victorian Studies*, iv (1961–2).

Thompson, A. F., 'Gladstone's Whips and the General Election of 1868', *E.H.R.* lxiii (1948).

Thompson, F. M. L., 'Land and Politics in England in the Nineteenth Century', *Transactions of the Royal Historical Society*, 5th ser. xv (1965).

INDEX

Men listed as M.P.s were Members in 1880

PRINTED IN GREAT BRITAIN
AT THE UNIVERSITY PRESS, OXFORD
BY VIVIAN RIDLER
PRINTER TO THE UNIVERSITY